FINANCES & THE END TIMES

Stephen R. Phinney

EXCHANGING LIFE PUBLISHING
P. O. Box 71 | Sterling, KS 67579

Unless otherwise noted, all Scripture quotations are taken from the *New American Revised Standard* (NASB), © 1960, 1962, 1963, 1971, 1973 by the Lockman Foundation, are used by permission.
Finances & The End Times

ISBN: 978-1-300-40499-6
Printed in the United States of America
Copyright © 2008, 2009, 2011 & 2012 by Dr. Stephen R. Phinney

IOM America
Exchanging Life Publishing
Kathy Hill, Managing Editor
P.O. Box 71
Sterling, Kansas 67579
(602) 292-2985

Library of Congress Cataloging-in-Publication Data
Phinney, Stephen Ray
Finances & The End Times /by Dr. Stephen R. Phinney.

© 2012
IOM America
Sterling Kansas

ACKNOWLEDGMENTS

My Wife Jane: Jane, my children and grandchildren have been the greatest influencers in my life when it comes to the topic of finances. For they have watched me learn, many times the hard way, the Biblical mandates and guidelines of managing God's resources and provisions. Each have been there as I dropped the ball, pick it back up and walk forward until I discovered the truth behind God's miraculous reasons for money, possessions, the end times and eternity.

Randy Alcorn: Randy, and his book "Money, Possessions and Eternity," have been used by God to stabilize my eternal view of finances. Randy, I thank you for being such a Godly and positive role model to me, my family, and our ministry and now through this book.

Jack Taylor: Over 30 years ago, while interning at Grace Fellowship International in Denver, I was given the privilege to get to know Jack and particularly his work "God's Miraculous Plan of Economy." That book not only changed my perspective on money but on how my identity is directly connected to my wallet. Thank you Jack once again for being a vessel of God to move the truth of stewardship to a new level of integrity.

Bill Gothard: I was given the honor to serve Bill by providing Christ as Life discipleship to him and his team in the late 70's. It was through this blessed opportunity that I was given the privilege to study and research his 18 principles on finances, which became the foundational outline for my book. I not only acknowledge Bill and his refined investment in Godly finances but I commend him for his life's work & devotion to Biblical truth and accuracy – a quality rarely seen in our world today. Bill, like many others, I thank you for providing resources to keep the next generation equipped in providing sound Biblical teachings to a hurting world – your legacy goes on in thousands of disciples.

David Jeremiah: Many people know Dr. David Jeremiah as a powerful teacher and preacher of the Word, but I know him as the man God used to open my eyes to the profound and simple truths of how money, the economy and the Antichrist are used by God to bring the final conclusion to the end times. I believe his book, "The Coming Economic Armageddon," is the most Biblically sound book written on the topic to date. Even though his book does not address the practical principles of finances, it was used by God to lead me to write a book that addresses both the end times and the practical helpful hints to managing money. I thank you David for having, and continuing to have, an impact in my life.

Kathy Hill: Affectionately referred to as "Edikat," Kathy is my Managing Editor. Together, through the years, Kathy and I have been blessed with the privilege of publishing many articles, booklets, books and ministry tools that have ministered to souls literally all over the world. My appreciation for her and her investment in eternal things is beyond the expression of words. God knew that my literary ministry wouldn't have a chance without Jesus using workers like Kathy.

Volunteers: Our ministry has been blessed with many volunteers, over 40 to date. Each of you knows who you are and the investment you continue to make in the Exchange Life Global Initiative! It is a privilege in Christ Jesus to work with each of you in order to advance the message of the Cross. Jane and I. the staff and Board of Advisers thank each of you!

TABLE OF CONTENTS

WHY THIS BOOK		7
INTRODUCTION		8
CHAPTER 1:	Knowing The Numbers	11
CHAPTER 2:	Nebuchadnezzar's Plan of Economy	15
CHAPTER 3:	Biblical Points of Financial Freedom	20
CHAPTER 4:	Seven Principles of Financial Freedom	25
CHAPTER 5:	Proof of Financial Bondage	28
CHAPTER 6:	Purposes for Money and Possessions	34
CHAPTER 7:	Purpose of Money	37
CHAPTER 8:	Confirming Direction	41
CHAPTER 9:	Multigenerational Giving	46
CHAPTER 10:	God's Miraculous Provision	51
CHAPTER 11:	Sixteen Lies of the Antichrist	56
CHAPTER 12:	Recognizing God's Correction	75
CHAPTER 13:	Ten Signs of Reproof	80
CHAPTER 14:	A Nation That Obeys Money	84
CHAPTER 15:	Choose This Day	80
CHAPTER 16:	Serving God Over Money	93
CHAPTER 17:	Establish a Pattern of Giving	97
CHAPTER 18:	Why Stay Out of Debt?	104
CHAPTER 19:	Debt Controls Our Past/Present/Future	110
CHAPTER 20:	Caramel Covered Rotting Apple	114
CHAPTER 21:	Learning to Be Well Content	119
CHAPTER 22:	The Rich vs. The Poor	124
CHAPTER 23:	Responsibilities of the Family	129
CHAPTER 24:	Special Care to the Poor	133
CHAPTER 25:	What is Your Standard of Living?	137
CHAPTER 26:	Humbly Suffer Need	140
CHAPTER 27:	Advertisement Junky	143
CHAPTER 28:	Resisting Sales and Bargains	149
CHAPTER 29:	The Super Saver	153
CHAPTER 30:	Being Held in Account	158

CHAPTER 31:	Money Matters to God	162
CHAPTER 32:	Poor Money Managers Are Thieves	167
CHAPTER 33:	Loaning to Loved Ones	171
CHAPTER 34:	Using Loved Ones for Financial Gain	174
CHAPTER 35:	Spend Money on Home Education	177
CHAPTER 36:	Financing Fun and Fellowship	181
CHAPTER 37:	Financing A Homespun Ministry	185
CHAPTER 38:	Price of a Working Mother	190
CHAPTER 39:	Money and a Good Name	196
CHAPTER 40:	Requirements of a Good Name	201
CHAPTER 41:	Destruction of a Good Name	206
CHAPTER 42:	Building Blocks of a Good Name	209
CHAPTER 43:	Mastermind of Reputations	212
CHAPTER 44:	Prayer and the Love of Money	215
CHAPTER 45:	Power of Money and Prayer	219
CHAPTER 46:	Praying for More Money	225

APPENDIX (Prayers & Additional Scriptures)	230
About the Author	233
Bibliography	234
Other Titles by Dr. Phinney	236

WHY THIS BOOK?

In today's Christian sphere, there are a myriad of different worldviews. Actually, many materials branded as "Christian" aren't even biblically based. Because we have grown up in a "Christian" culture, we tend to believe that many aspects of our culture indeed are Christian in nature. Sayings like, "God will never give you more than you can handle," "God helps those who help themselves," and "What doesn't kill you only makes you stronger" are tossed around as sound Christian advice in many circles. The problem is, they aren't biblical!

My family and I have been greatly blessed by IOM and the Phinneys. Their counsel, discipleship, and love have been invaluable to us because of the sound biblical foundation that underlies all that they say and do. When I am encouraged and/or rebuked by Dr. Phinney, I am done so with evidence in Scripture. His influence in my life has greatly shaped my worldview to a more biblical, Christ-centered perspective.

We first support IOM because we love the Phinneys and treasure them deeply in our hearts. We can't wait to correspond with them through text, phone, and email and are always looking forward to the next time we can physically be around them. However, the reasoning behind our support for IOM is much deeper than that. We support IOM because they believe and teach the Word of God, they don't water it down or sugarcoat it for approval by the masses. Their dedication to Truth has had a profound impact in our lives, and we want others to have that opportunity.

I believe as you read this book, your experience will be much like ours – one of an encounter with the Lord. I have an utmost respect and reverence for the Biblical topic of money, stewardship and the endtimes and I believe Dr. Phinney handles this topic with the care and guidance of the Lord.

Today holds the greatest opportunity to discuss this matter and we have found that the principles he presents in this book will probably be the best investment you have made this year!   -*Rob Cornelius, Florida, USA*

INTRODUCTION

God says the rain falls on the just and the unjust. For our reading benefit, we could easily say the "money falls on the just and the unjust." I cannot tell you how many times I have heard a believer ask, "Why is it that God allows the ungodly to prosper while Christians suffer with little?" The answer is found in reviewing the end-times. The way one spoils a rich kid is by allowing him to get sick from spoiling himself. As we look around at the end-times, we see an entire world prospering, but only for a season. As with all spoiled children, people of the world only focus on others to get what they want, in order to spend it on their own pleasures.

"You ask and do not receive, because you ask with wrong motives, so that you may spend it on your pleasures" (James 4:3)

Typically, God avoids supporting anything that gets in the way of true dependence on Him. Money has a way of leading people away from God, NOT to Him. God uses all things to lead each of His children to call out to Him – not, his banker. Believers are being awakened to the reality that their fight in life is not against flesh and blood, but the powers of darkness and the principalities of the air (Eph. 6:12). So many Christians today are deceived into thinking that what they see is what they are to battle. As the Lord draws near, we can be assured that our battle with the world, the flesh, and the devil will intensify. Worldly ideas of pop psychology will increase as the primary solution to our troubled minds. More rapidly than most of us realize, the questions people ask are based on worldly fables called philosophies of man. God is calling each of His children to call upon Him and He will deliver according to His divine Truth and Will.

Fear of confronting the enemy has held most believers back from boldly going before the throne of God regarding the temptations and afflictions of the enemy. God's greatest servants have always shared an appreciation of the magnificent power of prayer and the complete victory over Satan's kingdom available to all believers, through the mighty Person and work of our Husband, Jesus Christ.

The book of Ephesians is the New Testament handbook on spiritual, biblical prayer. Get to know this book like a handbook. The believer's emphasis in prayer must be upon a biblical and sound doctrinal approach to this subject. The Word of God recognizes that we encounter the three faces of Satan—the world, the flesh, and the devil. When a person becomes born-again, his/her relationship to everything in the physical, spiritual, mental, and emotional world completely changes. Since the believer is a citizen of heaven, he is given the power to face the enemy toe-to-toe. Scary? Well, look at it this way. Either we face him head-on or he will constantly be nipping at our heel—eating away our lives a little at a time.

To resist the limited power of the enemy, one must submit therefore to God first, then resist the evil one and he will flee. It is a promise given to us by God (James 4:7).

Because of our newly found relationship with God, all believers are marked targets for attack from God's enemy—Satan. Where does he seem to attack first? The love of money, of course! Since the love of money is the root of Satan, I would think this would be his main area of attack. If he can get the Bride of Christ to love money more than her Husband, believers will then begin to worship money and ultimately, Satan – a simple scam from a complex enemy.

Understanding that he is relentless in his attacks, believers must embrace the truth that the Father has given them a defense system—the power of prayer.

Believers have a supernatural resource of wealth and riches in the grace and gifts bestowed upon us in the Lord Jesus Christ. The Truths are ours for claiming power, position, authority, and total victory over Satan's world, which actually belongs to God the Father. The believer's victory over the enemy is absolute when the enemy attempts to use God's Truth to defeat us—his primary tactic of deception (2 Cor. 10:3-5).

It is important we learn to pray aggressive biblical prayers for family and friends who we believe are struggling with the bondage of the love of money. My experience as a counselor is those that ARE in bondage to the love of money can't read a book like this because of spiritual strongholds.

Even if you're not one of those, I suggest all readers to consider praying this prayer – it will make reading this book much more enjoyable. .

INTERCESSORY PRAYER FOR MONEY BONDAGE

My dear heavenly Father, in the name of our Lord Jesus Christ, I bring myself before You and ask for the Holy Spirit's guidance that I might pray in the Spirit as You have taught me. I thank You, Father, that You have sovereign control over all my money or lack of it. I thank You for the level of material possessions that you have placed in my life. In the name of the Lord Jesus and as a priest of God, I ask for mercy and forgiveness for the sins of the love of money, which grieve You. I plead the sufficiency of the blood of Christ to meet the full penalty that my sins deserve. I claim back the ground I have yielded to the enemy in my life, which I have knowingly, or unknowingly, given to Satan by believing the enemy's deception. In the name of the Lord Jesus Christ, I resist all of Satan's activity to use Your money or possessions that You entrusted to me. Exercising my authority, which is given to me in my union with the Lord Jesus Christ, I pull down the strongholds which the kingdom of darkness has formed against me with the love of money. I smash, break, and destroy all those plans formed against my mind, will, emotions, and even my wallet. I destroy in prayer the spiritual blindness and deafness that Satan has perpetrated against me.

I invite the Holy Spirit of God to bring the fullness of His power to convict, to bring to repentance, and to lead me into faith in the Lord Jesus Christ – my Savior. I cover myself with the blood of the Lord Jesus Christ and I break Satan's power to blind me to the Truth of God.

I believe that You, Jesus Christ, and the Holy Spirit are leading me to claim my freedom in You and I thank You for the answer to my prayer. In the name of Jesus, I joyfully lay this prayer before You in the worthiness of His completed work. Amen.

-Stephen Phinney

CHAPTER 1

KNOWING THE NUMBERS

This book will directly benefit those who care about the world of finances: personally, professionally, and politically. In my studies and research for a book I am writing (*Book of Revelation, the Final Frontier*), I am discovering many correlations between money, the end-times and personal suffering.

God has given us many of warnings in the Scriptures about being good stewards of what He has entrusted to us. Years ago, when I was in debt, God gave me this message for my journal:

"What is a steward? A steward is a simple messenger responding to a call to come to the Master's house to pick up a package for delivery. The messenger is to take the package with care, protection, and diligence and complete the mission given. The package does not belong to the messenger. It belongs to the Master. What is in the package is not as important as caring for the package and with all diligence, completing the mission with excellence. It is none of your business to know the Master's motives, what is in the package, or details of the person you are giving it to; but to simply deliver the package in the same condition that it was given to you. It is only a thief who will take from a package that does not belong to him. Stephen, this is why the enemy comes to kill, steal, and destroy. He wants all of My packages to arrive empty and destroyed. If I truly own everything, it means he will attempt to destroy everything I give you to steward. Do you see, My son? Being a good steward of what I give you does not have anything to do with being perfect with what I give you. It has everything to do with the mission I have placed behind the gift itself."

God has to simplify His Word for my frail and weak mind. This illustration was simple and to the point, but it worked. Two years later, I was completely out of debt.

There is a passage in I Kings that will become the foundation of this book.

"If the LORD is God, follow Him; but if Baal, follow him. But the people did not answer him a word" (1 Kings 18:21).

Elijah proposed a test to his opportunists. Two altars would be built. The prophets of Baal would call on their god and Elijah would call on his God. Whichever one answered by fire would be the one whom they would serve. I think you already know who won! If not, review 1 Kings 18:17-41.

In every generation, God's supernatural power will be tested against the competency of man and the Antichrist, as well as, their ability to fix the fix God has fixed on them. One of the tests that God places in our lives, if not the most frequent, is that of our personal finances. Stewardship communicates character - or lack of it. What we do with what God has entrusted to us will affect our eternal weight of glory. God challenges each of us to:

"Bring ye all the tithes into the storehouse, that there may be meat in mine house, and prove me now herewith, saith the LORD of hosts, if I will not open you the windows of heaven, and pour you out a blessing, that there shall not be room enough to receive it" (Mal. 3:10, KJV).

God is looking for men and women who will listen to His Words, obey them, and be willing to live out His financial principles. This includes demonstrating to a skeptical, unbelieving, indebted world that He lives and rewards those who diligently seek Him (Heb. 11:6).

So many Christians today spend hundreds and thousands of dollars to learn how to become ministers of the Gospel, but continue mounting massive debt. Only 6% of our churchgoers are 100% debt free. Men of honorable scriptural convictions will not only influence history, but will raise a new foundation of godly believers who will communicate the real Gospel of Truth.

I encourage all of us to embrace the following:

TEN PRIMARY CONVICTIONS OF THE WORD:

1. God alone is sovereign. The Word of God (Christian Bible) is His Divine and inspired Word and the final authority guide for my life.
2. My purpose in life is to seek God, Jesus Christ, and the Holy Spirit with my whole mind, will, and emotions and to build my life's objectives around His priorities.
3. My body is the living temple of God and must not be defiled by any lusts, doctrinal falsehoods, and/or idols.
4. I must attend a church that teaches the foundational Truths of the Word of God as His absolute Words to His children.
5. My life, wife, children, and grandchildren belong to the Lord. They are the vessels in which God delivers His Truth to the NEXT generation.
6. My daily activities and thoughts must never weaken the scriptural convictions of my brother and sisters in Christ.
7. My marriage, or plan thereof, is a lifelong commitment to God and to my spouse. I agree to only accept the Truth that one man + one woman = one flesh.
8. My personal, professional, and political finances are a trust from God and must be earned and stewarded according to the Divine Scriptures.
9. My words must be in complete and perfect harmony with the Word of God as I teach, preach, and live out the indwelt Christian life.
10. My mind and body's affections must be set on the things above in heaven, not on the things in or on the earth

We have so much to learn in our financial discussion. This is a critical topic! We are "spinning out of control" in personal, professional, and political spending; thus, creating debt like we have never seen in the history of the world. America's national debt grew 40%, from 1990 through the Bush administration. With the new Obama policies, it is projected to increase 180.6% by 2035. This means every American will need to be taxed a minimum of 50% of every dollar earned in order to pay this debt. By all given signs, America will NEVER be able to be debt free. If there is ever a global leader who calls in national debts, America will the first name called. What will happen to "in debt" nations? If we believe what the Bible says, the one who is in debt will become enslaved to the master financier. America and her church attendees are in deep trouble.

"But that slave went out and found one of his fellow slaves who owed him a hundred denarii; and he seized him and began to choke him, saying, 'Pay back what you owe' " (Matt. 18:28).

"Owe nothing to anyone except to love one another; for he who loves his neighbor has fulfilled the law" (Rom. 13:8).

CHAPTER 2

NEBUCHADNEZZAR'S PLAN OF ECONOMY

"The king reflected and said, 'Is this not Babylon the great, which I myself have built as a royal residence by the might of my power and for the glory of my majesty?'" (Dan. 4:30).

These were the words of the "great Nebuchadnezzar" - the man who had much pride and bondage when it came to the building of the "great Babylon." If you have been doing any reading in the book of Revelation, you will discover that Babylon will show its face one more time. This city has always been a thorn in God's side. It has and will again pride itself in wisdom, wealth, and power. In the case of King Nebuchadnezzar, he was turned over to a depraved mind for making such arrogant claims.

"Immediately the word concerning Nebuchadnezzar was fulfilled; and he was driven away from mankind and began eating grass like cattle, and his body was drenched with the dew of heaven until his hair had grown like eagles' feathers and his nails like birds' claws" (Dan. 4:33).

Why is God so offended by man or the Antichrist being so attached to wealth or external things? The answer is really too simple for the average mind to embrace. God knows that all who put their focus on wealth tend to forget Him. The other critical factor is people with wealth or excessive material things tend to think that it was by their hand. This ultimately provokes God to jealousy (Deut. 8:11, 17-18).

What means did God use to break Nebuchadnezzar of his pride? It would behoove all of us to review CHAPTER four of Daniel. But the simple overview is this: God took all the externals away from the king until he was able to give God all of the honor, glory, and credit for the existence of wealth. That took seven years!! Yes, seven years of eating and looking like a beast. Even though there are many parallels here regarding the Great

Tribulation of the Antichrist, God is making a clean and clear statement about man, money, and how he stewards it.

Thankfully, in Nebuchadnezzar's case, he repented and put his focus on the Creator - not all do that after such humbling. In fact, "Neb" himself lost his focus again. Wealth and possessions are seductive in nature, unless they are yielded to God. As with "Neb," God has three primary requirements when it comes to money:

GIVING: Being free from the bondage of the love of money begins with following the guidelines God laid out for us for biblical giving. When we give, it brings God into our finances in a personal way. It also provokes God to give more to the giver. " 'Give, and it shall be given unto you' " (Luke 6:38, KJV). Our new habit of giving must start with what the Bible calls our tithes and offerings of God. I will speak more about the difference between the two later, but for now; tithe is the highly requested 10% and offering is the above and beyond. Giving is the Christian's way of investing in heaven, kind of like heavenly stock, where " '...thieves do not break in or steal' " (Matt. 6:20). Giving also proves where our hearts are. So many claim they love Jesus; but until a person looks at his check stubs, it cannot be proven (Matt. 6:21).

RECEIVING: If we're good givers, then we are awesome receivers. Once God sees that He has a giver on His hands, He opens the doors of heaven to directly and indirectly bless him. He knows the more He gives this type of giver, the more he will give away. And the more given, the more needs are fulfilled by God. In order to be one of God's receivers, we have to be in tune with God Himself. Personally, I believe God is intimately close to givers and receivers. He knows where His messengers of answered prayers are available. Keep in mind that the measurement we give is most likely the measurement we will receive (2 Cor. 9:6).

ACCOUNTING: It is one thing to be a giver and receiver, but it is an entirely different thing to be a manager or an accountant (one who keeps adequate track and account of what is coming in and going out). Everything we eat, spend, save, or invest is to be held in account to God for how we use each and every penny we have. Many do not even realize that the Word is clear as to what we should spend His money on. I will reveal these areas later; but for now, know that He is detailed. God told us in His Word to flee from those who would waste our time and take our money. He instructs us to use great care and prayer in what we purchase. Why? It is His time and money we are stewarding. As we wisely steward small things, He will entrust more, or the greater, to us later (Luke 16:10).

Being freed from the "Nebuchadnezzar plan of economy" is realizing true wealth and prosperity come only from God. He is the One who chooses the measurement of wisdom, wealth, and health. If we think that we can get rich quick by our own education, investments, or practices, we will become the victims of our own schemes. God will soon bring a lesson upon us much like that of "Neb." It may not be as extreme as with Job or King Neb, but that will be God's choosing (Deut. 8:18).

Freedom comes when we are committed to God's Divine purpose of money. The purpose of money is not to bring us security and protection. These are reasons that many use, but these reasons don't have caps or ceilings to them. The purpose of money, for most, is to breed independence - not having to lean on our fellow brothers and sisters for aid. Money is for full dependence on God. It demonstrates God's love and power over us. When we have money, we become stewards. When we become stewards, we have to depend on the One who is going to tell us how to steward it (Matt. 6:30). That's it!

We will know we are free when we can recognize false worldly financial concepts. Actual freedom comes through restraints - God's restraints. Freedom is in being a steward, in fact, a bond-servant. Remember:

"For he who was called in the Lord while a slave, is the Lord's freedman; likewise he who was called while free, is Christ's slave" (1 Cor. 7:22).

One of the toughest elements of being a freedman is embracing God's discipline. All of those times we sin by not bringing application to God's mandates, God allows riches with sorrow. He even allows the success to devour our investments. Many times we go on a lifetime search for this wealth and never find it (Hag. 1:9). We turn into a bitter old person, asking the same old question: "Why me?" God loves His children and a father who loves his children will discipline them. Many times, God's discipline is in hiding the prosperity of our dreams.

Being financially free is by the willpower to serve God rather than money. What we serve proves the location of our love. This is why God said, "For the love of money is the root of all sorts of evil" (1 Tim. 6:10, KJV). Notice it is not the money that is evil, but the love of money. God rarely makes a big deal about the money in the world, but rather the love of such things. This is what provokes God to being jealous (James 4). In the end-times, Satan wants people to serve him through their love for power, money, and success. Not to insult your intelligence here, but HIS PLAN WORKS. Without question, this is one of the reasons why God sends His Son for a Second Coming.

Did you know that being out of debt is a biblical requirement? It is! God asks us not to be in debt to any man or institution. Most debt is the result of our disregarding God's eternal guidelines and not being willing to wait on Him for His supernatural provisions. I know the violation of this Truth quite well. I grew up an impatient child who got tired of waiting on anyone, let alone God. I understand the struggle to stay out of debt at all costs. The person or institution we are indebted TO becomes our master. In the end-times, if we are in debt to man or his human institutions, we will be forced to pay the piper (Satan) in one facet or another. This is the connection with money and the end-times that many believers do NOT want to look at. I have even known some "Christians" to go into deeper debt because the "Antichrist" is right around the corner. Do what is moral, legal, and of God, to get OUT OF DEBT (2 Kings 4:7).

Another principle I learned about being free financially is learning how to embrace the suffering of poverty, as easily as, embracing abundance. Learning to accept abundance is kind of a joke to me. I know there are some who find it difficult to have money and material gain, but not this boy. I find the loving embrace of abundance fun and enjoyable. Now, learning how to embrace the suffering of poverty? No, that is not an easy embrace for me. When God decides to abase me, I starting thinking thoughts like: "God is angry at me," "I am not as good as other Christians," or "There is 'unconfessed sin' in my life somewhere." This is one of the toughest messages of Truth for me to hear, even though I know it is required of me to do so (Phil. 4:12).

CHAPTER 3

BIBLICAL POINTS OF FINANCIAL FREEDOM

The impulse to buy is something most people struggle with, but few realize the bondage that accompanies these impulses. The marketplace provides many opportunities to trap us into becoming undisciplined in our shopping habits. We want, we see, and we buy. Many times it can be as "candy coated" as the purchase of candy itself. God wants us to have the discernment of the Holy Spirit in all of our purchases. The problem is as old as the garden itself. One example is when Eve purchased fruit with the price of her soul. We must reject all that appeals to the lust of the flesh, the lust of the eyes, and the pride of our lives (1 John 2:16).

SWINDLERS: The first and foremost problem that needs to be addressed is that of recognizing and rejecting the swindler himself, Satan. No being knows the marketplace better than our enemy. He is a shrewd businessman who uses earthly swindlers to place people in bondage; primarily, those who make claims to be in the kingdom of God. A swindler, as depicted in man's reality, gives very few evidences of his deception. A con artist is usually friendly, personable, and enthusiastic about his product or in how we can make large sums of money by "buying into" his product. His, or her, technique is to get us to focus on the business aspects, or profits, of our demise. But, God wants us to focus on the warning signs of deception. If we do this, He will find a way to reveal the way of deliverance from such tricks of the trade.

"To deliver you from the way of evil, from the man who speaks perverse things" (Prov. 2:12).

God will deliver us, but we must know the ways of a swindler. History has proven that women tend to struggle with impulse buying over that of men. I am not convinced this is the case in God's reality. Men tend to purchase BIGGER toys that cost more; whereas, women do tend to make smaller purchases more frequently. What is true, about both male and female, is statistics prove that female salespersons are more difficult to turn down - at least for men. This problem roots itself as far back as the Garden of Eden. Why did man say, "yes" to the dress? Well, that is the million dollar question isn't it? Because of Adam defaulting to Eve in the garden, men have had a generational problem of saying NO to women. Through the years, many men have told me that if the little woman is happy, I am happy. The price tag of Adamic default is enslavement. Adam was disciplined by God because of this single factor of disobedience.

"Then to Adam He said, 'Because you have listened to the voice of your wife, and have eaten from the tree about which I commanded you, saying, "You shall not eat from it"; Cursed is the ground because of you; In toil you will eat of it All the days of your life' " (Gen. 3:17).

I am by no means putting the blame on the woman - on the contrary. In fact, I am putting full responsibility on the man. God disciplined Adam because he listened to the voice of his wife. The weaknesses that Adam and Eve suffered while in the garden are the same weaknesses men and women struggle with today. Satan is still appealing (tempting) through the woman to appeal to the default of man - giving into the voice of his woman instead of listening to God. That puts the responsibility on the man to establish clear boundaries of spending for his entire household. Women are to spend freely within those boundaries. It is an issue of patriarchy, leadership, and roles defined by the Holy Scriptures.

I have counseled hundreds of men through the years. I have found that most men buy their BIG toys because their wives spend on impulse. It is almost like he uses her shoe shopping as an excuse to buy his boat. Therefore, he continues to allow her cycle of small purchases to justify putting his family in debt; thinking that she will then be silent when it comes to his impulse purchases. This is not godly logic or reason.

I know that we can't pigeonhole every family into this formula, but overall, I personally believe it is a primary tactic Satan uses to place the whole family into self-justified debt.

BEST BUY: A significant part of financial freedom is getting the best buy; but getting the best buy is not always justifiable to God. Getting a godly good buy requires taking the time and effort to do research. That means walking away from purchases that do not measure up to the predetermined standards of God. It means knowing exactly what we want and seeing if it meets the checklist of how to spend God's funds. "God buys" are a result of a disciplined life of knowing God and His guidelines of spending.

RECORD KEEPING: God is an accountant! If He records every word that proceeds out of the mouth of man, surely He is recording how we are spending, or stewarding, His resources. If we are to prosper under the guidelines of heaven, we must be wise in our planning, be diligent in working towards the purchase, and be accurately recording the expenditures of God's bank account. If the Master, God, would require an account of His resources, we will be ready to present an accurate account of how we spent our Master's investment.

LENDING: Another downfall of many men is lending with interest and cosigning on loans of family and friends. If borrowing money makes us a servant to the lender, then lending money to a family member, or friend, forces that one to become our servant. Since we know the Word of God is True, we need to be very careful about making slaves out of our familiar loved ones. When we "loan" - we need to loan under the guideline of not expecting it back. If our new servant pays us back, we are blessed. If he doesn't, in our eyes and in the eyes of God, we are still free. Loaning money for profit is NOT a biblical principle. Our world hinges on this lie and it IS what makes the world turn, at least financially. It is also the technique the Antichrist will use to prosper the world's economy and place the people in a slave position to him. He will be the banker in the up-and-coming global banking system. God expects us to give to those who are in need. Cosigning and loaning with interest means bondage to the one for whom we signed, and also potential bondage to the lender (Prov. 31:10).

DOMESTIC: Those who discover God's miraculous plan of economy prepare their homes for education, medical recovery, care for elderly family members, housing, food, and clothing. The patriarch of the family will spiritually train up his children and grandchildren to be the providers for their own homes, without going into debt to do it. This will certainly require the leader of the home to become educated on the guidelines of spending, according to the Word of God.

GOOD NAME: One of the most difficult principles of financial freedom is choosing a good name, rather than great riches. Scriptures show us that broken commitments, secret sins, not taking care of widows, dishonoring parents, and taking revenge are just a few of the sins that get in the way of God caring for His children. If a person of pride thinks he can care for his family without the Hand of God, He most likely will allow the downfall of such thinking. God would prefer for us to put our emphasis on being of good reputation or having a good name - one that the generations who follow us can inherit (Mal. 3:10).

PRAYER: A principle that continues to be a struggle for me in financial freedom is in knowing how to receive resources from God through prayer. God is pleased when His children call on Him for help. Like most humans, when wealth increases or even stabilizes, it becomes easy to cease depending on God. This proves our independence and reason for wanting the wealth to start with. The answer is a dependent prayer life with our Lord. Pray about everything, and I mean everything - a habit that challenges me to this very hour (Eph. 3:20).

PARTNERSHIPS: A temptation many men struggle with is becoming a partner in ventures to gain prosperity. The reason why this is not biblical is because it places both parties in enslavement to each other. When one falls, they both fall. It is deceptive thinking that the end justifies the means. Even though the technique works well in the lives of the wealthy, the average business and family usually end up in bankruptcy over such unbiblical practices. It would behoove us to review Daniel 1:8.

LAZINESS: There is no other way to label those who invest in get rich quick schemes. Attempting to live and prosper without working for it is viewed by God as a slothful workman. He placed the discipline on man to work by the sweat of his brow (Gen. 3:17-19) and this is what He expects from the man. Unless it is an inheritance or gift, anything short of this is strongly classified by God as irresponsible living. Over the years of being in ministry, I have had countless offers to join multilevel marketing firms, and in every case, God has led me back to Luke 12:19.

LISTENING TO OUR WIVES: For many of us who are married, listening to our wives (not obeying) can be one of our greatest challenges. Many domestic financial disasters are a result of not paying close attention to our wives' female instincts. Our wives function much like the Holy Spirit; they have an uncanny ability to discern what is not wise for the family's welfare. She is our "one flesh" and we, as men, cannot function without our helpmate, unless we are in full dependence on God. God gave her to us to complete us - even in our financial decisions.

INHERITANCE: True financial freedom comes to a household when the patriarch knows how to pass on a spiritual, relational, and financial heritage. God gave us the principle of inheritance in order to pass on the Truths of His kingdom into all areas entrusted to man. From what we can discover in the Word, His purpose of inheritance is to strengthen family life and multiply the investments made by the previous generation. These are God's vital signs for the family: spiritual education, more children, health care, provisions, caring for the elderly, family businesses, and having a good name. Proverbs 13:22 states "A good man leaves an inheritance to his children's children." Also, in Proverbs 20:21, "An inheritance gained hurriedly at the beginning will not be blessed in the end." For many of us, we may not be able to leave a boatload of cash, but we can teach our children's children how to manage the inheritance of God's resources - whatever that might entail.

CHAPTER 4

SEVEN PRINCIPLES OF FINANCIAL FREEDOM

God has established financial principles for us that are not optional. These are requirements, if we want to live according to the Divine Word of Truth. If we choose NOT to live by these simple principles, we will view money as a personal possession that can be obtained by our own resources. The result is a self-reliant life. This gains the attention of a God who cares enough to put us in our place.

If we view these seven principles as mandates, we will find long-term freedom in our personal, professional, and spiritual lives.

SPIRITUAL ACCEPTANCE: A man or woman who does not accept his position of being a child of the King, or rejects the ways of God, will suffer with overwhelming feelings of inferiority or self-rejection. The negative results of not accepting our position in Christ will often, if not always, manifest itself in self-indulgent spending, or attempting to buy things in order to make ourselves feel better about our "self-image." This is the most common form of spending. This can show its ugly head through the purchases of boats, cars, clothes, houses, or by merely "bargain buying." Knowing who we are in Christ, our identity, is critical in being a godly steward of the King's resources.

EMBRACING AUTHORITY: It is impossible for a man to steward God's resources, if he does not place himself under God's authority. This is practically done through submitting ourselves to a mentor whom God has entrusted to oversee our life, as well as, to the written Word itself. This is why He gives us spiritual fathers/leaders. People make independent decisions with their finances because they ARE independent. Most of the people in our postmodern world are not quick to place themselves under God given authority. Authority has become a "nasty" word in our society. Followers tend to only submit themselves to "authority figures" who have proven themselves to be wise. That is not the original mandate given to us by God. Authority is authority. If the authority asks us to do something immoral, ungodly, or illegal, we are to say NO to that particular request. If the authority is asking us to do things that are within the boundaries of the Word of God, we are to wholeheartedly say, "YES" and go do it quickly. This is a practice lost within the pages of biblical living. The only way to break a man of independence is through dependence. "Servants, be submissive to your masters with all respect, not only to those who are good and gentle, but also to those who are unreasonable" (1 Peter 2:18).

A CLEAR CONSCIENCE: People who suffer with a foggy conscience will lower the standards of God to fix their morbid beliefs. Once this occurs, a lifestyle of compromise will fill that follower's heart and mind with worldly fables. He can then only trust in his own judgment in how to spend God's resources. The guilt experienced by a believer like this will spur him on to spending even more on fruitless possessions. First Timothy 1:19 says: "Keeping faith and a good conscience, which some have rejected and suffered shipwreck in regard to their faith." A man or woman, who does NOT have a clear conscience, will end up with a shipwreck of a life.

FORGIVING: The terms forgiveness, reconciliation, and restoration are biblical words to define a balanced Christian life. They are also financial terms used in the Word. To accurately handle ourselves with the Gospel of Jesus Christ, we must accurately handle our resources from God in like manner. If we are quick to forgive an individual for hurting us, we will be just as quick to forgive his debt against us. God graced us - we grace them. If we do not forgive others for the pain that has been trusteed upon us, we certainly will not be quick to forgive them of what they "owe" us.

Financial freedom equals spiritual freedom. It is that simple. God has also called us to the ministry of reconciliation. This not only means going to our brother to reconcile hurt and blame, but it also includes our finances. To truly reconcile with someone, we must count the cost of loss. We are required by God to let go of any harbored feelings or debt we hold on him. Restoration is restoring the relationship by whatever means God requires of us. Many times, this means releasing someone of the debt against us. The terms of the Gospel are the same terms used in financial freedom (Heb. 12:15-17).

I HAVE NO RIGHTS: Only the meek inherit the earth. A meek person is one who has yielded his rights to demand what is right. He quietly waits for the Hand of God to demand His rights. Meek people diligently work to wait for the right time to proclaim the Words of God - not demand it! Those who demand payment are never satisfied with the payment. They usually "want a pound of flesh" as they say. Proud people (not meek) enjoy watching people squirm their way into humility. Most lenders find more gratification in the enslavement they create, than they do in being paid in full. This is a technique the Antichrist will use in the final days. Debt equals bondage and bondage requires service.

MORALITY: Anyone who violates God's principles of morality, sooner or later, becomes a slave to immorality. I believe the primary reason for all the immorality in the world today is because people refuse to respect, and obey, the laws of God's morality. Being moral is not a sexual concept. Being moral is accepting the purity of the guidelines of a moral and just God. As long as the people of this world violate God's principles of finances, there will be immorality. You can count on it.

CALLING: People wander because they have no purpose and people without a purpose have not embraced their calling. When a man or woman of God commits himself to God's holy and righteous purpose for being on this earth, he will properly steward the resources of God. This can only happen when you and I seek first God's kingdom and His righteousness. Once we do this, He will add all these things in and unto our lives (Matt. 6:33).

These are the seven principles of financial freedom. I am not one for making promises UNLESS the promises are backed by our Living God. This I do promise: if we adhere to these seven principles, we WILL be financially free.

CHAPTER 5

PROOF OF FINANCIAL BONDAGE

It is easy to see if someone is in financial bondage. One's life becomes an outward view of an inward problem; a person radiates the reflections of a rebellious life. These people, me included, are lukewarm at heart and filled with bitterness and resentment. When we encounter a bitter person, in most cases, we are seeing a person who is in debt spiritually, relationally, and oftentimes, financially. As a counselor, or discipler of people, I hunt for nine primary symptoms of bondage.

INSECURITY: People who are not secure in who they are in Christ are typically building their identity around another person – usually someone who has more than they do. Their minds are fragile. They are easily offended and quick to defend their position of bondage. They fight being confronted with the pride of self, which is not only annoying to the observer, but to God Himself. They are a people who are difficult to counsel, due to their unwillingness to be told what to do. These people are so focused on being like another, that they defend the humanness of their graven image, rather that embracing the image of God. Insecure people are defenders of self and rebels of wisdom. They find great comfort in hiding behind the mask they wear. To put it simply; they are living out the lives of someone who is more prosperous. These people parrot the lives of those they admire. They DO NOT know who they are.

FILLED WITH FEAR: Individuals of fear are so aware of their environment that they work to block out the things that upset their existence and reason for living. They tend to make decisions based on the externals of life, including finances. Fearful people surround themselves with comfort foods, material possessions, and relationships that won't upset them. They seek to have a quiet life, but rarely find it. When they obtain the results of their fear, they become fearful all the more. First John tells us that fear involves punishment. These people are quick to punish themselves with their own fears and are equally quick to punish others who move or change things around in their environment. Fear is NEVER satisfied! It has no boundaries and finds no rest – no matter how hard one tries. The only solution to fear is love. God's perfect love chases fear out of a person's life. Usually their fear has a price tag connected to it. This price tag is in spending money on things that subdue their fears: drugs, food, clothing, etc.

ANXIETY: Anxiety is the emotion of unpredictability. Those who suffer with this are always concerned about the details around them, almost like they are infringing upon the sovereignty of God. They think that if the circumstances were different – they would be different. As you might know, it doesn't work. It only complicates their lives and brings on more feelings of anxiety. These people are difficult to deal with, let alone live with. If you are one of these anxious people, you even find it difficult to live with yourself. People of anxiety do not trust - not in themselves, nor others. They tend to be "controlling" and act out of control. Their methods are madness and they tend to live in a constant state of anger. Financially, they spend to feel good – many times referred to as shopaholics. Even though this is not always true, the tendency is there.

INSOMNIA: God said NOT to let the sun go down on our wrath/worries (Eph. 4:26). Worries are always worst when we lie down to sleep. The sounds of distractions are minimal, the tugs from the needy are in waiting, and the environment becomes conducive for the enemy's favorite place – darkness. Having debt when we lie down to sleep is like going to bed without forgiving someone. It will cause tossing and turning the whole night through. When I read this verse, I oftentimes hear these words in my head: Stephen, do not let the sun go down on debt - spiritually, psychologically, or financially.

A LACK OF THANKSGIVING: OK, maybe you are in debt! Are you thankful for it? I am not saying we should be thankful for going INTO debt, but rather being thankful for the opportunity for God to teach us through the debt. When, and only when, we are thankful for the circumstances God has allowed in our lives, will He deliver us from them - one decision at a time. Thankless hearts are greedy hearts. Plus, a thankless person spends his/her days worrying and complaining about the consequences of their own fruitless decisions of getting into debt to start with.

ENSLAVED TO THE ANTICHRIST: People, who are in debt, are led around by a ring in their noses – the ring being their debt and the one leading them around being the lender. Debt works like this. If I loan you something that belongs to me, that something binds us together by way of a "ring-in-nose" relationship. By you accepting this "loan," you give me permission to intrude into your life. What you are claiming as your own isn't really yours – it's mine. I just let you say it is yours to make you feel comfortable with being my slave. I'm just giving you permission to hold what is mine, until the terms of agreement have been completed. A good example of this is "would-be homeowners." Almost every "homeowner" that I know talks about "their house" like it is their house, when we both know that in the ugly world of debt, it belongs to the bank. Even if we are one of the 0.08 % that has paid off the house in full, the ground under our feet doesn't belong to us. Most do not know, nor do they care to know, the truth about true home ownership. The ownership package only includes the first six inches of soil under the house. I had a client, a few years ago, come to me so angry he was "fit to be tied." The government was forcing him to sell his house that he had worked his entire life to "pay in full." Not only that, they were offering him a ridiculously low price. I had the unpleasant responsibility of telling him that by way of federal mandate, he only owns the first six inches of soil on his land and that if he didn't move his house, or sell it, he would lose his complete investment. I further explained that the federal government requires all states to reinforce this federal mandate just in case the government needs that land, i.e. in his case, a freeway. In reality, the individual states or the federal government can take possession of every inch of land bordered out as the United States of America, IF, they deem it necessary to do so.

What if the federal government itself was in so much debt that it, too, could not pay its lenders? What becomes, or is, the collateral? I can assure you it is NOT the Monopoly money being printed by the US Mint or the gold hidden in the closets of our US Treasury. It is none other than the land under our feet. I really hope you see the covert scheming that has been going on by the primary enemy of God. Have we become so deluded as to think Satan was sleeping when the laws of the lands were established? Most assuredly not; it was while we were sleeping that these laws were established! He has been proactive in every form of government: worldwide, 24 hours a day, seven days a week, without one blink of sleep or slumber. He knows that sheep cannot be led to a slaughter without "cattle rails" – policies and laws. Since over 90% of our world's countries have adopted this type of land law, I personally believe the Antichrist will gain ownership of the planet by way of these established laws. Any historian worth their salt knows what I just said is true. Why? History proves itself over and over again. Policy proves ownership and ownership grants permission.

So many Americans are concerned about being enslaved to "BIG Government," but I say that our very own government better examine the ring in its own nose. If indeed our government has a ring (debt) in their own nose, a couple of questions are begging to be asked: What master is leading the American people and where is he taking us?

Does the global climate policy of land ownership bother you? Consider this: God is the originator of this mandate. Satan is just doing his normal thing and replicating what God does. You see, this way, it is guaranteed to work. Satan wants debt: individually, nationally, and globally. Without debt, he cannot rule!

There is nothing we own that cannot be taken from us – nothing. Even if we did find something completely free of debt, God could take it away in a heartbeat. After all, He is the owner of ALL – and that ALL includes us, our banks, and even Satan.

JEALOUSY: Individuals who suffer with debt are typically a jealous people. Jealousy, according to the Greek, is "the passion of ownership of; or possessing an exclusive right over a person, place, or thing." God is the only being that has this exclusive right over people, land, and their possessions. When humans attempt to use the verbiage of rights of ownership, they provoke God Himself to be a jealous God (Ex. 20:5). Usually when I bring up this topic around lukewarm "Christians," I'm accused of the sin of semantics. From what I read in the Holy Scriptures, provoking God to jealousy by making claims of ownership is a big deal. In fact, one of the Hebrew names of God is Kannaw – "Jealous One." So, I just tell them to go ahead and take ownership of some person, land, or possession; while we all watch to see if the God of the universe manifests the mandate of His name – the Jealous One.

Do people not see that well over 50% of our market purchases are based on jealousy? This principle is SO true that the manufactures design their products to be insured/guaranteed for about one year. The upgrade mentality is based on the lies associated with jealousy. Why put guarantees on products for more than a year when statistics prove that the consumer replaces the product within the first year of "owning" it? Manufactures are not necessarily making products of lesser quality because they want to "cut corners." It is usually based on the principle of marketplace jealousy.

ARROGANCE: Why would indebted people be arrogant, when they have nothing to claim as their own? James 3:14 says, "But if you have bitter jealousy and selfish ambition in your heart, do not be arrogant and so lie against the truth." According to these truths, when individuals are suffering with jealousy and selfish ambition, they are arrogant and actually lie against the Truth. Arrogance is the main characteristic of a liar and a thief. This is why arrogant people love the gamble of debt – they "borrow" from Peter to pay Paul. They typically purchase things to give the appearance of being wealthy and secure, even if it takes getting a loan to do it. In God's reality, they are only one lawsuit away from poverty.

Do you know the percentage of loans granted today that are for the purpose of paying debt? Yes, you read me correctly; more debt, usually with a higher interest rate, to pay for delinquent debt. I don't know the percentage, but I can assure you, it is the biggest chunk of national debt represented in the private and government sectors. I have asked two separate global economists how I can get my hands on "pie charts" from the international banks stating such statistics. In both cases, they said that these numbers are "privatized." For those of you new to this term, that means the International Banking System is owned by the private sector (nongovernment) and thus, any governmental loans released through their bank becomes privatized – individually owned. Who are these private sector people and why do they call the shots on the value of the coin? I'll tell you why; the lender calls the shots. Secondly, almost every country in the world is in debt to the International Banking System. If the IBS ever calls in their loans, there will be a bunch of nations having the carpet (land) pulled out from underneath their feet.

If you're like me, you will find a lot of this global finance stuff a bit hard to believe. My observation is that history tends to repeat itself and that there is nothing really new under the sun. I am not speaking so much as a prophet, but more as a historian. If history does indeed repeat itself, the global climate is about to change.

BITTERNESS AND RESENTMENT: These two words do an adequate job of describing someone who loves money more than they love God. Why? Those who love money are playing with the root of all evil. Those who play with evil are challenging God to remove the very possessions that form idolatry. Once they catch on to the fact that God is removing these objects, they become resentful and bitter. If you would take the time to read through the book of Revelation, you will discover an unstoppable mission of God to remove all the earthly things from the people, obedient and disobedient alike. He does this in order to observe where the people place their glory. A reasonable mind would think disobedient people would get the message and repent; but they don't. They actually become more resentful and bitter – which is something the love of money has the ability to do.

DISILLUSIONMENT: When indebted people attempt to use money to fill their unhappiness or obtain that possession, they quickly discover their purchase didn't make them feel any better. Not only that, they soon realize the additional debt has only added to their feelings of disillusionment and despair.

CHAPTER 6

PURPOSE OF MONEY & POSSESSIONS

Have you ever worked diligently to get out of debt, just to find yourself back in debt several years later? I have - three times. Debt mentality is a dangerous place to live. God said that the natural mind cannot understand the things of God. In fact, He goes on to say that the things of God are foolish to Him. Any mind that is not reconciled unto God, either through Salvation and/or by way of walking after the Spirit, is a mind that is in debt. The way that a man manages his finances is a direct reflection of his relationship with God – or lack of it.

"But a natural man does not accept the things of the Spirit of God, for they are foolishness to him; and he cannot understand them, because they are spiritually appraised" (1 Cor. 2:14).

THE NATURAL MIND: The tragedy of a man with a natural mind is he will NEVER be able to understand the wisdom of God. It will be easy for him to get into debt and stay there his entire life. He will resort to his own understanding and experiences to live from one master (financer) to another – constantly borrowing from Peter to pay Paul. The man with a natural mind is unsaved and has never asked Jesus Christ to come and live within his mortal being. His mind is easily seduced by earthly, natural, and demonic ideas.

"But if you have bitter jealousy and selfish ambition in your heart, do not be arrogant and so lie against the truth. This wisdom is not that which comes down from above, but is earthly, natural, and demonic. For where jealousy and selfish ambition exist, there is disorder and every evil thing" (James 3:14-16).

The sobering reality is that the natural man cannot understand God's purposes of spending money. Honestly, he won't even really care. If it doesn't make sense to him, why would he want to live it out? So if you are an unsaved reader, good luck; because luck is all that you have going for you. If you pray that the Spirit grants you understanding, you might just be asking for Salvation. In that case, you might want to consider reading the prayer in the Appendix at the back of this book.

SPIRITUAL MAN: This is a person who has asked Jesus Christ to come into his mortal body through Salvation. Christ lives in him and he lives in Christ. Because of this truth, the indwelt Spirit gives guidance and understanding to the Word of God. If a person does not have the indwelling Spirit living and breathing IN him, he has zero capacity to understand any of the elements of God (1 Cor. 2:14-15). Not one jot or tittle. The spiritual man can hear words of wisdom and become overwhelmed with a peace that God is speaking to him through the words, printed or spoken. This is because outwardly spoken words become a witness to inwardly spoken words through the enabled power of the Holy Spirit. This is one of the GREATEST blessings an indwelt Christian possesses, once saved!

This all reminds me of the story of Elijah and the brook. Elijah was asked; OK, commanded by the Lord to flee to a brook in the wilderness. At first this sounded a bit strange to me, but as I read on, I soon realized that God was about to show him the most powerful principle of heaven – God is in charge. He obeyed God, and as a result, he was protected from the wrath of that horrid Queen Jezebel. God then miraculously fed Elijah by ravens every morning and evening (1 Kings 17:1-6).

If it wasn't for Elijah knowing the difference between hearing the voice of God versus his own, God only knows what would have happened. It was during those months that God not only saved his life from the wicked queen, but He freed him from severe despair – or as the world calls it, depression. Through this provisionary time, God delivered rest for his body and MIND. God lavished him with intimate fellowship and he experienced daily proof that God was his provider. God revealed His miraculous plan of economy right in front of Elijah's eyes. By the way, this was during a time when there was severe feminine in all the land.

Sooner or later, the brook dried up. Although God could have miraculously kept the water flowing, He used this apparent "lack of provision" to move Elijah from this comfortable place to the widow Zarephath. Again, as expected, Elijah obeyed God. Later, he understood God's purpose for such a move.

I don't know if you remember the story, but the widow Zarephath had only enough food for one more meal. God directed Elijah to instruct her to make a meal for him first. When I first read this story, I really thought Elijah was being quite selfish. But later, I saw the reality of what God was doing. The widow obeyed, and because she did, God miraculously multiplied her food. In fact, God's blessing and provision lasted for over a year, until the famine was over. Again, her ability to hear and obey allowed her to embrace and understand one of the most important financial principles: When we give our first fruit to God, He causes the remainder of our assets to meet our needs – even if it takes supernatural multiplication to do it.

CHAPTER 7

PURPOSE OF MONEY

Financial bondage is an immediate consequence of NOT understanding the rhyme and reason for God's purpose of money. Contrary to most opinions, the purpose of money is not to provide security, build independence, or to create power and influence in the community. God's purposes are much more basic.

FIRST PURPOSE OF MONEY: BASIC NEEDS

It really doesn't take much to sustain human life: food, clothing, and shelter. The odd thing is that in a world filled with wealth and prosperity, these are the three greatest needs found in almost every country in the world. Did you know that one in seven people in the United States live below the poverty level? In a world of 2.1 billion people, almost half the world's population is living on less than $2 a day, each barely staying alive. That is unbelievably disturbing, but very telling.

Since this is the case, where is all the money going? Believe it or not, the money is being stored up for the Antichrist. Those in world power, like the G-20 World Council, actually work to keep the majority of the world's population below the poverty line. It is a political maneuver that has been used since the days of the first kings. The grave appearance being offered by the Global Finance Commission is that of a growing economy and prosperity; when in reality, poverty is actually getting worse. The United States is at the top of the pile when it comes to the "appearance of wealth." But in reality, 88% of Americans are one paycheck away from living on the street. Why? - because of debt. Debt makes a person look and feel like he is living above the poverty, but the truth is – most of the 88% are enslaved to the 12%!

Hebrew culture shows us that the one who provides is the master. This is a simple principle God gave His people to live by, since the beginning of man's time. God demonstrates His loving care by setting Himself up as the provider of all the resources needed by man to live. Jesus said:

" 'Look at the birds of the air, that they do not sow, nor reap nor gather into barns, and yet your heavenly Father feeds them. Are you not worth much more than they? And who of you by being worried can add a single hour to his life? And why are you worried about clothing? Observe how the lilies of the field grow; they do not toil nor do they spin, yet I say to you that not even Solomon in all his glory clothed himself like one of these. But if God so clothes the grass of the field, which is alive today and tomorrow is thrown into the furnace, will He not much more clothe you? You of little faith!' " (Matt. 6:26-30).

Paul imparted these words of counsel to pass on to the churches through Timothy:

"If we have food and covering, with these we shall be content" (1Tim. 6:8).

PRINCIPLE ONE

ESTABLISH DEPENDENCE: God is quick to reveal His mandate that man must depend on Him for all things. Since the beginning of man, mankind has worked to become independent of God. Because man was born independent of God, this has become man's greatest weakness – a desire to be self-sufficient. Because of sin, man has an innate passion to be his own boss. From this self-justified position, man tends to use God like He is some kind of a slot machine, by praying for prosperity and wealth. However, God doesn't respond to such prayers. Instead, He told us to pray, " 'Give us this day our daily bread' " (Matt. 6:11). He is the only One who really knows that daily needs produce daily dependence.

PRINCIPLE TWO

LOVE LIFE: When God's children fail to embrace their need for a Provider, they lose their love for the One who provides for them. God created us to depend on Him for all of our needs and that comes through an overwhelming desire to need Him. There is only one way we can be complete. It is in Christ - apart from Him, we can do nothing.

"And in Him you have been made complete, and He is the head over all rule and authority" (Col. 2:10).

Christ is head over all rulers and all authority. This includes all the global leaders who think they have ownership of the world's economy. When the Israelites were in the wilderness, God taught them to look to Him for daily food, shelter, and even the sandals for their feet. He orchestrated this dependence by drying up any and all avenues of self-provision. There was no food or water to be found, no matter how hard their self-sufficient efforts tried. This practice is one that God makes use of to this very day. Every man, rich or poor, is commanded to depend on God as his Father–Provider. If we study the Scriptures, we will find God using famines throughout the Word to help His people get refocused on Him.

PRINCIPLE THREE

DEVELOP GRATITUDE: Being thankful in all things is probably the most challenging mandate God has given His people. Having a thankful heart for the basics is a blessed by-product of contentment in Christ. However, we all begin to lose our "rest in Christ" when we compare what we have with that of others, particularly those of the unsaved world. Our expectations dominate our minds' focus. If we expect from man, we will most likely apply pressure on man to provide for our needs. If we expect from God, we ultimately will place our focus on our relationship with God. We are created to love the one who provides for us. If it is man, we will tend to love man more than God. If it is God, we will certainly love God more than man.

PRINCIPLE FOUR

LIVING WITHIN OUR MEANS: Contentment only comes by living within the boundaries of a God-ordained budget. Being content in Christ, and His fulfilling of our basic needs, helps us resist the ongoing onslaught of temptations that we are not truly content unless we buy some new "thing." God's reality is - a contented child of God feels wealthy because he knows he already possesses more than he needs for daily living.

"But godliness actually is a means of great gain when accompanied by contentment" (1 Tim. 6:6).

PRINCIPLE FIVE

ENJOY WHAT WE HAVE: Always being in the "want" destroys our ability to truly enjoy the things that God has given us. This occurs when we are moved to focus on the things that we THINK GOD SHOULD give us, rather than on what we do have. The Word of God calls this covetousness. God wants us to enjoy the possessions He has allotted for us. He finds great delight in watching His children have fun, laugh, and make use of the things He gives us.

These are the five principles of purpose number one (basic needs): dependence on God, having a deeper love life with Him, being grateful for what we have, living within our means, and enjoying what He has given to us. Be assured - when all five of these come into play, we will be well content with money being a provisionary factor of our basic needs.

CHAPTER 8

CONFIRMING DIRECTION

Throughout biblical history, God has used the lack of provisions (money) to guide and direct His people in His given pathway. There are times He uses the abundance of provision, or the lack of it, to confirm His direction for our lives. A classic example of this is the purchase of a car, but not having the funds saved to purchase it. For godly stewards, we can safely see that until God provides the funding, it is not His will for us to buy the car. For each of us who have fallen into the poor steward mentality: we see, we want, we pray, and we go into debt to get it.

SECOND PURPOSE OF MONEY

CONFIRM DIRECTIONS: Let's say that we do have the funds set aside to make the purchase. Is it God's will for us to go ahead and buy? Not necessarily! God bases the "yes" on one simple factor - Is it a true and real need? This, too, can be subjective. We humans tend to rationalize our decisions based upon what WE think is a need, rather than what God calls a need. In order to discover that which God calls a real need, we must embrace all of the stewardship guidelines of the Word. An example is buying a used car instead of a new one. Buying a new car is not necessarily a sin; whereas, purchasing a good used car may be more in line with God's rules of stewardship.

One of the first symptoms of indulgent purchases I watch for in myself, as well as in others, is that of impatience. People who "buy on the spot" with large purchases tend to justify their indulgences. Those who carefully weigh the "pros and cons," walk away, pray, and then decide, show due diligence unto the Lord.

"Rest in the LORD and wait patiently for Him; do not fret because of him who prospers in his way, Because of the man who carries out wicked schemes" (Psalm 37:7).

Let's examine the five building blocks of this particular purpose of money.

PRINCIPLE ONE

BUILDING FAITH: God has made a commitment to clothe the grasses of the field, which are alive today and tossed into a pile of rubble tomorrow. Will He not much more clothe you and me if we have increasing faith (Matt 6:30)? The Lord seems to move upon the lives of those who show or demonstrate faith. I really think many times God wonders where and what we are doing with our faith. He implores us to have faith in His name, which has more strength than that of any man. God is more interested in revealing Himself from faith to faith and thus, requiring of us to live by such faith. Faith is evidence of believing in unseen things – the things of God. God expects us to use our spiritual gifts according to the grace given to each of us and to exercise them according to His Divine will.

Faith helps us to discern what God wants to accomplish in and through our pocketbooks. All of us should carefully weigh how each dollar is spent, according to how it ultimately benefits God's glory and kingdom. Once God gives us clear direction on how we spend His money stewarded to us, we then can have confidence toward God in our daily walk with Him.

When we patiently wait on the Lord for spending, and saving, we are given the privilege to see the bigger blessing He has for us. Most of us settle for "cheap" things because we are unwilling to wait on God to provide us with what He has stored up for us. An example is buying that car on credit when God may have a vehicle ready to be given to us. There are so many material possessions just lying around, waiting on God to move the heart of a giver to answer the prayers of one of His needy. But most simply do not have the faith to see the blessing arrive. Waiting develops and establishes faith.

PRINCIPLE TWO

LORD OF LIFE: How often do you and I proclaim that Jesus is the Lord of Life, while we live like we are the lord of our own lives? Lordship is only confirmed when we are obedient to the moving of God's hand and respectfully honor the limitations that He places on our lives. A person who has plenty of money stored up will find it very difficult to see God's guiding hand. This is not to say that all those who are blessed with large sums of money don't hear God. But the norm is those of wealth tend NOT to seek the kingdom of God first, before they spend. Statistics prove, the more one has, the less one depends on God. Because of this, God gives significant warnings to the wealthy:

"Instruct those who are rich in this present world not to be conceited or to fix their hope on the uncertainty of riches, but on God, who richly supplies us with all things to enjoy" (1 Tim. 6:17).

PRINCIPLE THREE

PROTECTION: Have you ever noticed that no matter how much God blesses us, we want more? I certainly do! As we look into biblical history, we see God providing many men with everything they need, plus some. In a few short CHAPTER s, they are crying out for more. This all started in the Garden when God gave Adam and Eve absolutely everything they needed to enjoy life. Satan came along and put the thought in both of their minds that they can have much more, in fact, that they could have as much as God. From that day forward, man's sinful bent has pushed him to see, want, and get. I believe this was Satan's method of madness to set the world up for debt mentality. The enemy is well aware of God's principle of not being in debt to any man and that man becomes a slave to the one who holds his debt. Upon this principle, we have the financial system of the Antichrist. He also knows the wealthy fall into temptations and snares easier than the poor.

"But those who want to get rich fall into temptation and a snare and many foolish and harmful desires which plunge men into ruin and destruction" (1 Tim. 6:9).

We find in God's continuous history that He tends to use His people's need for money to protect them from falling into the temptations and snares of Satan. We always need to remember that need creates dependence and dependence forms relationship.

PRINCIPLE FOUR

BUILDING PATIENCE: Patience is not something we learn, practice, or memorize. Patience is a fruit resulting from a dependent lifestyle and appropriation of allowing Christ to live His life through us, as indwelt believers. Patience is evidence of a mature Christian, who is in the habit of depending on Christ "in them" to make the decision through them. We are told this fruit comes to maturity through tribulation (trials).

"For what credit is there if, when you sin and are harshly treated, you endure it with patience? But if when you do what is right and suffer for it you patiently endure it, this finds favor with God" (1 Peter 2:20).

Financial hardship, no matter what level of the economy we live in, tends to be viewed by each of us as suffering. Due to this weakness of man, God uses the lack of funding to produce a trial. Through this trial, God causes the fruit of patience to bloom.

PRINCIPLE FIVE

TRUE RICHES: In God's mind, there is a major difference between earthly riches and heavenly riches. Mankind gets caught up in the worries of the world and the deceitfulness of riches. Once this occurs, desires for other things enter in and begin to suffocate the Word in the believer. God works diligently to place the Word within the hearts of His children. Yet, there are some of us who allow these profound principles of God to be choked out by the worries of wanting more money and the pleasures of life. The end result is not fruit of the Spirit.

Why would God entrust heavenly riches to someone who is unfaithful with the use of unrighteous wealth? He not only can't, He won't. God measures the amount of heavenly riches according to how the man is faithful with the earthly riches. He is known for starting out by placing small things in our hands, to see if we will be faithful in stewarding them according to His Word. If we are, He entrusts much to us. That is how it works. We cannot truly understand the riches of His glory unless we understand the importance of properly stewarding the things of the earth. God wants to impart to us the depth of His riches in sound wisdom and knowledge of Him. These are the things God finds admirable in His children – not the amount of money we have stored away in our piggy banks.

"But whatever things were gain to me, those things I have counted as loss for the sake of Christ. More than that, I count all things to be loss in view of the surpassing value of knowing Christ Jesus my Lord, for whom I have suffered the loss of all things, and count them but rubbish so that I may gain Christ" (Phil. 3:7-8).

In conclusion, we have learned that God is more interested in: our level of appropriated faith, who is "lord" of our lives, protecting us from the snares of the devil, developing the fruit of patience in us, and being able to trust His children with true riches. It is through these elements we find confirmation of God's given direction in our lives.

CHAPTER 9

MULTIGENERATIONAL GIVING

There is a plan of economy presented in the Bible that is not influenced by recessions, depressions, topless inflation, or the value of the global dollar. It is God's financial plan and economy that is of utmost importance. It involves the control and management of all of the affairs of mankind, including man's choices on how to spend his money. God's plan of spending has very little to do with the benefits here on earth, but rather building up "eternal weight of glory" in His heavenly bank account. In the end, God's plan actually reconciles with all of earth's treasures, resources, capacities, as well as, man's role in stewarding each. This must include the eternal purpose in the mind of God, as He created all. In other words, money should reflect the face of God. If it doesn't, the earth and all that is in it, including mankind, become out of balance.

THIRD PURPOSE OF MONEY

MULTIGENERATIONAL GIVING: Man's economic systems collapse because he has been selfish in his spending and has failed to include in his "economic principles" those matters vital to the kingdom of God – the Four Purposes of Money. Man's greatest error in handling money is that he has not reckoned with his responsibilities to the God of the universe, the One who made all resources. The other big mistake is that mankind does not reckon his responsibility to human kind – marriage, family, community, state, nation, and then, the world. Instead, he has trafficked his available resources to his immediate advantage and then has the gall to sign the name of Christ to his reasons of insanity. The result has been the destruction of resources necessary to the whole family of God.

Our level of giving reveals our depth level of spirituality with our Heavenly Father. If we have a greedy eye, our whole worldview will be greedy – what I get out of life. On the other hand, if we are giving and generous, our worldview will not only be a biblical worldview, but it will be transformational.

"A man with an evil eye hastens after wealth and does not know that want will come upon him" (Prov. 28:22).

" 'Do not store up for yourselves treasures on earth, where moth and rust destroy, and where thieves break in and steal. But store up for yourselves treasures in heaven, where neither moth nor rust destroys, and where thieves do not break in or steal; for where your treasure is, there your heart will be also. The eye is the lamp of the body; so then if your eye is clear, your whole body will be full of light. But if your eye is bad, your whole body will be full of darkness. If then the light that is in you is darkness, how great is the darkness!' " (Matt. 6:19-23).

The price for mankind NOT obeying the foundational rules of God's plan of economy is very high. If you and I do not submit ourselves to the Matthew passage, the whole balance of economy will be out of order. Plus, this is what will give the Antichrist the opportunity to place God's children in slavery once again. Paul reminded the wealthy Romans of this:

"Contributing to the needs of the saints, practicing hospitality" (Rom. 12:13).

God specifically calls each believer to care for his fellow Christians before giving outside of His fellowship. The way most Christian churches function is to suffer their own congregation by allowing their own members to go hungry, while at the same time spending the "lion's share" of the offering on staff benefits, programs, and overseas missions. When God said to us that those who don't take care of their own household are worse than unbelievers, He wasn't joking. The same principle applies to the church. Meeting the needs of our own household first is what unites the body of Christ.

PRINCIPLE ONE

CHRISTIAN ONENESS: Back when the New Testament church was being formed, the Jews had no social dealings with the local Gentiles. God's remedy to this dilemma was to set forth a severe famine, which caused many Jewish Christians to suffer. The result – Paul challenged every Christian Gentile church to collect an offering for his Jewish brothers and sisters. God used this offering to dissolve the spiritual, psychological, and physical barriers that had been built out of ignorance. As expected,

God's plans of economic equality worked miraculously. Paul later shared the dynamics of this happening to the Corinthian church.

"At this present time your abundance being a supply for their need, so that their abundance also may become a supply for your need, that there may be equality" (2 Cor. 8:14).

TO DEMONSTRATE TRUE CHRISTIANITY: Where there is greed – there is war! It is impossible to pursue peace with all men, when one party is seeking to care for its own needs according to its own advancement. The confusion and consternation among the global society are but a magnification of what is going on in the hearts of the people who live within its boundaries. The Antichrist has always sneaked in when the deceit of man's system of greed corners itself; when his rudeness of selfish rules of economy has finally imprisoned him. Just as greed marks the foreheads of unbelievers, so does giving mark the hearts of true indwelt Christians.

When a true Christian gives from the integrity of his heart, God grants him special desires and powers to multiply all of his efforts in his day-to-day life. This is why it is so important for a Christian to give, even if he doesn't "feel" like it. God sees each and every sacrificial gift offered – particularly when it hurts the most!

TO ACTIVATE A THANKFUL HEART: Giving to the needs of fellow Christians causes others to thank God for providing for them. Each and every gift offered puts the other in a position of glorifying God directly and indirectly. This is why giving activates expediential growth in the body of Christ. Giving empowered by the Holy Spirit not only meets practical needs, but results in an overflowing tide of thanksgiving to God and to the one who does the giving.

"You will be enriched in everything for all liberality, which through us is producing thanksgiving to God" (2 Cor. 9:11).

One of the basics Christianity is that praise and thanksgiving are the building blocks of growing Christians - God's Church.

BROADENS THE POTENTIAL OF GIVERS: Does God have anything to say about the world's greedy and political plan of economy? Without question He does! He has always had something to say about mankind supporting the Antichrist's system of debt mentality and greed investments. It always amazes me how some "Christians" justify using their tithes and offerings to invest in ungodly and corrupt stocks/companies that use their profits to murder babies, kill off the elderly, or worse, proclaim their hatred toward our God. All this and they don't feel one ounce of guilt; all under the banner of "providing security for their family and/or future." God warned us about stealing from His investments throughout the Old Testament, but one passage in particular clearly marks this warning.

" 'Will a man rob God? Yet you are robbing Me! But you say, "'How have we robbed You?" In tithes and offerings. You are cursed with a curse, for you are robbing Me, the whole nation of you! Bring the whole tithe into the storehouse, so that there may be food in My house, and test Me now in this,' says the LORD of hosts, 'if I will not open for you the windows of heaven and pour out for you a blessing until it overflows' " (Mal. 3:8-10).

Dear reader, you can push this passage aside, call it legalism, continue to spend God's money on personal gain, and continue investing His resources (your money) in earthly treasures that provoke Him. BUT, you will never be able to escape the mandates of the New Testament. If you're like me and you carefully study the New Testament regarding the issues of spending, you will be shocked as to how much is required of the followers of Jesus Christ when it comes to the topic of giving. But I can assure you – it is FAR beyond the 10% spoken of in the Malachi passage (Matt. 19:21; Luke 12:33-34).

Jesus said to him, "If you wish to be complete, go and sell your possessions and give to the poor, and you will have treasure in heaven; and come, follow Me." (Matthew 19:21)

"Sell your possessions and give to charity; make yourselves money belts which do not wear out, an unfailing treasure in heaven, where no thief comes near nor moth

destroys. "For where your treasure is, there your heart will be also. (Luke 12:33-34)

God's plan of economy cannot be explained by man or his rules of engagement! It is my prayer that both you and I find it impossible to respond to these simple principles with a casual shrug of the shoulders. I desire that these writings will challenge and change the lives of each reader. At the same time, I hope these works are imperiling any lifestyle that disregards the will of God as man's supreme ruler/measuring stick and cause an encounter, resulting in partaking in God's perfect plan of economy!

CHAPTER 10

GOD'S MIRACULOUS PROVISION

Did you know a person can evaluate the condition of a man's heart by looking in his checkbook? It's true – the Word tells us that a man's heart is where his money is. Therefore, when we tug on a man's wallet, we tug on his heart. This is a principle God makes use of every single day. Most men (and women) believe they are the owners of their own wealth and if they are broke, they are the first to blame another for their poverty.

God made us for Himself, empowered us to live life, and gave us the resources to sustain His kingdom work here on this earth. When any of us attempt to take ownership of His allotted resources, it is classified as stealing or robbing from His storehouse (see Malachi 2) and provokes Him to being a jealous *God*. It is IN Him that we live, move, and have our very being, which should certainly include our earthly treasures.

God is the owner and the presider over all the wealth and material possessions in this world – even the collectables that the Antichrist presently has stored up for himself. When we compare apples with apples, that piece of paper in our pocket, called a dollar, has little or no value. The only reason it is "burning a hole in our pocket" is because man has placed some kind of sumptuous value upon it. Did you know that one community of Revelation's Seven Churches is responsible for placing value upon a coin/paper? The township of Thyatira was the first to "invent" money. This community was also known for being the first to enslave women to work outside the home, in order for the men to advance in wealth. In fact, the definition of Thyatira means "worthless feminine thing." This community became one of the primary targets for Satan to establish his Beast (global economy). The aftermath of the work Satan accomplished in this community is still at work in our wallets today.

Let's face it, God is a miraculous God and His economy is everlasting. He wants to show His people His reality and power, to both the saved and the unsaved world. One means by which He has chosen to do this is through His miraculous provision of money, possessions, and generosity.

First of all, we need to define miracle. It is a "supernatural power, being birthed through a natural event, with precise timing to bring glory to God." It is a normal, natural, and neutral work of God. Miracles are not big, oversized events or happenings to God. They are His normal day- to-day works. For example: When a child of God prays about a special financial need and an unexpected and unsolicited gift is handed to him or her by one who did not know about the need, the supernatural power of God is revealed from glory to glory.

" 'Bring the whole tithe into the storehouse, so that there may be food in My house, and test Me now in this,' says the LORD of hosts, 'if I will not open for you the windows of heaven and pour out for you a blessing until it overflows; " (Mal. 3:10).

God rarely grants permission to "prove" or "test" Him in anything, except in His plan of economy. There are five wisdom principles in the Word to explain this Truth. Let's take a look at them.

PRINCIPLE ONE

TO BUILD TRUST: Many times, "Christians" try to worship God and Satan at the same time. Since "the love of money is the root of all evil" (1 Tim 6:10, KJV), the walk from money to Satan is short and oftentimes destructive. When we don't trust God with His money in our possession, we activate God's judgment; so He proposes a test on us. The test involves us facing the two altars we claim to serve. God wants us to choose the god we believe serves and cares for us the best – God or Baal (Satan). Whichever god answers by supernatural power ought to be the one in whom we should worship and place our trust. Therefore, when God says, "Test Me in this," He really wants us to see with our own eyes which god really backs Truth.

As seen in the story of Elijah (1 Kings 18:21-40), the prophets of Baal cried out to their god all day long and nothing happened. Then Elijah prayed a prayer of trusting faith and God sent fire from heaven. This heavenly fire consumed the offering, the altar, and the water around it. God is serious about proving His trust, in His own ways.

PRINCIPLE TWO

TO PUT TO SHAME OTHER GODS: I doubt any true indwelt Christian would disagree that money is the "god" of our present day. This "greenback monster" has become an idol in the lives of some of the finest prophets of our day. I remember counseling the limo driver of the most televised evangelist the world over. The confessions that rolled out of this man's mouth blew me away: limos, Bentleys, gold plated furniture, renting complete hotel floors, etc. That is the short list. Even though I was appalled, I knew the love of money would bring evil upon that ministry – and it did.

As the world of the Antichrist is expected to seek after money, God desires for HIS children to seek after Him FIRST. Then He will provide all they need afterwards. Seeking after God involves building our lives, motives, heart, and activities around Him, His Son, and the Holy Spirit.

PRINCIPLE THREE

TO PURIFY OUR MOTIVES: A requirement of God, in order for us to experience His supernatural power in finances, is actively seeking Him with a pure heart through selfless motives. Review this verse:

"If I regard wickedness (vanity) in my heart, The Lord will not hear" (Psalm 66:18, parentheses Hebrew).

Vanity is the result of spending money on making oneself look "better off" than he really is. That, my reader, covers a lot of ground. God warns us about vanity. I believe, He will not answer the prayers of those who refuse to listen to this appeal. The requirement for God's miraculous control in our financial affairs is super-powered by our willingness to let Him examine our hidden motives.

PRINCIPLE FOUR

LEAD UNSAVED TO CHRIST: Money, or should I say, the management of money can be a powerful tool to lead an unbeliever to Christ. When believers are "right" with the Lord, and each other, and when each of them are truly experiencing God's miraculous works of provision, nonbelievers are drawn to Jesus and the local churches they attend. How a nonbeliever can look at a minister who spends his donor dollars on mansions, limos, and gold plated furniture, and not question the leader's authenticity of God is beyond me.

A couple of years ago, I was given the budget details of a church in Phoenix, AZ. Then I was shown the annual budget of one of the countries in Africa and how the annual budget of this local church could care for the entire budget of this poverty-stricken country for four years. The gentleman said, "Wait, there's more." He went on to show me the statistics connected to the local churches regarding debt (i.e. building loans, corporate credit cards, etc.). The results confirmed that just the churches in America show more debt than 2/3 of all the countries in the entire world combined. That boggles the mind a bit. Needless to say, that should sound off an alert in the minds of true Christians. It is no wonder why the TRUE Gospel is being silenced in America and why the Emergent Church is showing its ugly head.

PRINCIPLE FIVE

TO GLORIFY THE NAME OF THE FATHER: God is NOT going to share His glory with Satan. It's that simple. Since the love of money is the root of all evil, those that love money (Christian or not) are covertly glorifying Satan instead of God. I know this sounds a bit blunt, but it is authentically real and true. God the Father does great things for His children, so they can pass the real Gospel of His Son on to the next generation. God wants future generations to glorify Him not only in times of need, but when times are abundant in resources. If His children will glorify Him in times of trouble, they certainly will give Him all the credit and honor for the "good times" as well.

"Offer to God a sacrifice of thanksgiving and pay your vows to the Most High; Call upon Me in the day of trouble; I shall rescue you, and you will honor Me." But to the wicked God says, "What right have you to tell of My statutes And to take My covenant in your mouth? "For you hate discipline, and you cast My words behind you. "When you see a thief, you are pleased with him, and you associate with adulterers. "You let your mouth loose in evil and your tongue frames deceit. "You sit and speak against your brother; you slander your own mother's son. "These things you have done and I kept silence; you thought that I was just like you; I will reprove you and state the case in order before your eyes. (Psalm 50:14-21).

We must ask ourselves where our sacrifice of thanksgiving is, are we paying our vows before God and do we call on the name of the Lord when we are in trouble – or do we in our panic reach for that credit card?

CHAPTER 11

SIXTEEN LIES OF THE ANTICHRIST

True indwelt Christians live in two worlds at the same time – man's reality and God's reality. The world of the Antichrist is seeking to drag us into bondage by how we individually choose to handle our money. He, Satan, is not able to control our lifestyles unless he is able to enslave us through debt. His system of economics always pulls us down to earth with the same force that the earth calls our bodies to the grave with each day. It is like gravity; it will have its way unless another force overrides the laws of gravity. This is where the realm of God comes in.

The world, the flesh, and Satan are always applying their pressures to conform the image of the Beast, which is Satan's economic system. The Antichrist is gifted at denying and disregarding the Truths of the Holy Scriptures, which are foundational in God's world of economy. As long as the enemy gets us caught up in his sensory world, we are not apt to be investing, by faith, in the unseen world in which God lives. In fact, it actually takes a "born-again" experience for mankind to partake in the unseen world.

Even though it is difficult to believe, the resources of the believer are NOT found in the seen world. For those who have "put all their eggs in this one basket," they are in for a BIG surprise.

"We are destroying speculations and every lofty thing raised up against the knowledge of God, and we are taking every thought captive to the obedience of Christ" (2 Cor.10:5).

People who invest in the seen world will form speculations (lies) and arrogant thoughts, which rise up against the mind of the Lord. There are sixteen primary lies which arise against God in the visual world. Let's review them:

LIE ONE – BECOMING SUCCESSFUL

This idealism is manifested when an individual chooses to believe that he, rather than God, is the source and abler of his wealth.

"Otherwise, you may say in your heart, 'My power and the strength of my hand made me this wealth.' But you shall remember the LORD your God, for it is He who is giving you power to make wealth that He may confirm His covenant which He swore to your fathers, as it is this day" (Deut. 8:17-18).

My guess is there's nothing more that provokes God to prove He is a jealous God, than for a man to profess that his financial area of life was, or is, attained through his own strength and power. Unless a "body member" is put into the position of depending upon the full Body of Christ to live "hand to mouth," I personally do not believe one can experientially accept this Truth.

LIE 2 – THERE IS NO EXCUSE FOR A CHRISTIAN TO BE POOR

This is the most touted statement in the Emergent movement of prosperity doctrine. This group of "believers" uses God like He is some type of a slot machine. They grab and quote Scriptures to further their dementia of demise. God does not care if a man is rich or poor, no matter how much he may "name it and claim it." He desires to use the "widow's mite" just as much as the rich man's towers of grain. These emergent "Christians" don't even take the time to realize that two-thirds of the world's population lives on less than $2 a day. A little over 75% of the world's population will never have the resources available to them to even live out the prosperity doctrines. Western theology can really be ridiculously stupid at times. The Lord is into having his Bridal members for His Son to gather often, to share what they have in common, and to depend on each other for all their basic elements of living.

"The rich and the poor have a common bond; The LORD is the maker of them all" (Prov. 22:2).

LIE 3 – WE DETERMINE OUR OWN FINANCIAL CAPACITY

We need to discover and embrace the Source of our supply! The Father arranged a very miraculous system of provision by mandating the Holy Spirit to come and live WITHIN the born-again believer. This system of function puts the new believer in the position of looking inward for his resources, instead of depending on an external world that has been temporarily yielded to the Antichrist. Jesus is the same in us as He is in heaven - right now, this very minute. He has brought into our mortal beings the total wealth of heaven. With that comes the same rule of engagement of spending or stewardship that presently exists in heaven. Wealth in heaven is for the Divine purpose of glorifying God and expanding the radiant beauty of His vast domain. Remember when Paul said that we have been blessed with every spiritual blessing in heavenly places in Christ Jesus (Eph. 1:3)? This is the kind of wealth the Lord is asking us to embrace; not the kind our mortal flesh can muster up, in order for our retirement years to be more predictable.

Do you believe in a Sovereign God? Do you believe that sovereignty means "a great, mighty authority who controls all?" Do you believe it is possible God would actually destine the level of wealth or poverty that people are to steward? Or, are you like the "prosperity doctrine" people and dare to tempt God with the thought that all Christians should be independently wealthy? If you are of the latter, you are in for some serious struggles and hardships that DO NOT further the Gospel of Jesus Christ. God does not want us "wheeling and dealing" for resources or security. If we decide to do this, He will multiply our sorrows!

"The sorrows of those who have bartered for another god will be multiplied; I shall not pour out their drink offerings of blood, nor will I take their names upon my lips" (Psalm 16:4).

LIE 4 – A RESPONSIBLE CHRISTIAN CAN ACHIEVE

This lie is the clearest satanic example of the stubbornness of the Antichrist. One of the most common questions asked by True indwelt Christians is, "Won't Satan ever realize that he is doomed and will lose in the end?" Satan lives by the popularized phrase: "If you first don't succeed, try, try again." Through his own morbid stupidity, the Antichrist believes in the false idea he can achieve success and happiness independent of God. Since this is the banner that flies in the face of God on a day-to-day basis, he (Satan) works to deceive mankind into thinking that he, too, can achieve financial independence and true happiness apart from God. If we think God will support this kind of "pull ourselves up by our bootstraps" mentality, we are under the full deception of the Antichrist and his clever system of bondage. God will never support anything that puts confidence in human ability, rather than giving proper recognition and dependence to Himself and His enabling power. Anytime a Christian sets his focus on fleshly endeavors, death is sure to follow. But, those who desire life and peace passionately pursue setting their affections on looking inward at the Holy Spirit ("holy storehouse").

"For the mind set on the flesh is death, but the mind set on the Spirit is life and peace, because the mind set on the flesh is hostile toward God; for it does not subject itself to the law of God, for it is not even able to do so" (Rom. 8:6-7).

Plans are often thrown into gear in great times of need or in overwhelming demand. Sometimes in the middle of that great demand, we discover the former source of our supply can no longer be depended on. Flesh always gives the impression of competency; but in reality, it fails us every time. In fact, God causes our flesh to fail us!

Our flesh is arrogant, independent, and full of lies. BUT, I will say, our flesh is competitive and stubborn (I'm unwilling to say "quite"). Because of this, God typically allows our flesh to spiral downward, to the bottom of the barrel. Flesh hates depending upon others for help and guidance. Flesh, money, and personal identity all go hand in hand, in man's mind. In God's economy, Spirit dependence, money, and identity in Christ, all form true and honorable stewardship. As we review the next two lies of the Antichrist, keep God's formula for a successful economy in mind.

LIE 5 –BECOME FINANCIALLY INDEPENDENT, SO I WILL NOT HAVE TO LOOK TO MY CHILDREN, OR OTHERS, FOR HELP

This is the lie that has re-formed our global view of family. It is through this lie that abortion, euthanasia (killing the elderly and weak), and retirement homes were birthed. Family integrated churches, multigenerational missions, and interdependent family life are all functional doctrines of the past because of this western theological blunder. The new postmodern emergent beliefs of independence and self-life fulfillment now dominate our postmodern pulpits and media marketplaces. Adult "Christian" children now consider additives or beliefs such as "assisted suicide" (euthanasia), elderly placement, elderly social welfare (Medicare/Medicaid), and any other program that will relieve them of the financial burden of caring for weak and elderly family members.

The reality is Satan DOES have us "over a barrel" – so to speak. He has been working for centuries to reverse the family model of God: heads of homes, women working at home, and children honoring their fathers and mothers. Paul states:

"But as for you, speak the things which are fitting for sound doctrine. Older men are to be temperate, dignified, sensible, sound in faith, in love, in perseverance. Older women likewise are to be reverent in their behavior, not malicious gossips nor enslaved to much wine, teaching what is good, so that they may encourage the young women to love their husbands, to love their children, to be sensible, pure, workers at home, kind, being subject to their own husbands, so that the word of God will not be dishonored" (Titus 2:1-5).

Sound doctrines should be at the base of every Christian family. Paul is openly telling us to speak the things which are fitting for sound doctrines. He goes on to show us what the basics are in family life:

- Older men are to be: temperate, dignified, sensible, sound in faith, in love, and in perseverance.
- Likewise, older women need to be reverent (holy) in their behavior: not gossipers, nor enslaved to much wine. They are to teach what is good so they may encourage the young ladies: to love their husbands, to love their children, to be sensible and pure, to be workers at home, to be kind, and to be submissive to their own husbands. This is so THE WORD OF GOD WILL NOT BE DISHONORED.

What this tells me is that Satan is going to work the global society to be opposite of the structure and mandates of God's design for the family. He did this in order for the people to ultimately feel trapped when asked to carry out these rules of engagement. The postmodern "Christian" church now reads these verses like this:

But as for you modern Christians, speak the things which are fitting for modern Christianity; which are fitting for those who need to feel God's love. Your older men should be peaceably put aside for retirement, have a dignified death, be sound financially, lovers of themselves, and able to let go of the next generation while living. Older women are to be reverent and honoring of the decisions of their children, releasing themselves from parental correction, allowing their children to learn from their own mistakes, and shutting their mouths when it comes to the affairs of family life. When it comes to encouraging their daughters to be "workers at home," they need to remember that those mandates only worked in "biblical days" when the environment supported such beliefs. With the issue of challenging their daughters to love and submit to their husbands – well, in the postmodern world, that's simply abuse. With the whole issue of "honoring the Word of God" – keep in mind the Word can be interpreted many different ways (my paraphrase of the "opposite" of the Truth in Titus 2:1-5).

Satan was probably laughing as I wrote this because if anyone knows the trap which has been created through the generations, it is he. Women of the postmodern society rarely can experience the privilege of being "workers at home" and homeschool their babies. Their husbands and fathers are off committing the family to more debt, which usually requires "putting the little woman to work" in order to keep their "credit report" from going into the dumper. So, when it comes to having their elderly parents depend upon them for daily living – well, it just is not "financially feasible." What is the solution for such a dilemma? Simple – send one's children off to a godless government school, allow the local church to train the children spiritually, put those elderly parents in a county retirement center, and continue "putting the little woman to work." Meanwhile, when the children grow up, they appropriate their training by being as independent as possible and moving away from their parents, while grandma has to work in the local community kitchen until she drops like a rock. Don't you just love the American way?

Abundance is for the wanting of those who are in need. When any individual, or family, loses sight of that, spiritual poverty settles in.

"At this present time your abundance being a supply for their need, so that their abundance also may become a supply for your need, that there may be equality" (2 Cor. 8:14).

LIE 6 – AS LONG AS I CONTINUE TO PROVIDE FOR MY FAMILY, THE EXCESSIVE FAMILY TIME SACRIFICED JUSTIFIES IT

Really? Ask any woman committed to family life what she thinks about this lie. This lie is meant for the postmodern Christians with the priorities of work, money, friendships, recreation, family life, community, church, and then extended family (maybe). I used to think working parents who steal time from family life were doing it because of a work ethic. But, as I watch the youth of today, I see more of an addiction to material things. Not long ago, we could put the full responsibility, and blame, on the head of the home. But, the biblical principle of "headship" is no longer a societal norm. I see the responsibility still upon the man of the house, but place the blame equally upon the woman. In postmodernism, women love being away from the home. Considering staying home to care for the children and/or her husband creates an overwhelming sense of suffocation and restraint.

The real and actual needs of a family are not material blessings, sports, recreation, or family fun times, but rather, spiritual leadership. No amount of money can buy back the time and leadership sacrificed to keep family members "happy."

"Then He said to them, 'Beware, and be on your guard against every form of greed; for not even when one has an abundance does his life consist of his possessions' " (Luke 12:15).

God would rather have the parents spend their time, effort, and money on restoring hearts and relationships.

"He will restore the hearts of the fathers to their children and the hearts of the children to their fathers, so that I will not come and smite the land with a curse" (Mal. 4:6).

There is an unspoken rule operating in God's reality that necessitates problems, needs, and demands. God only supplies when there is a heavenly defined need, NOT in times of want or self-imposed need (debt). For every righteous need, there is a righteous supply for that need. For every self-imposed need, there is a self-imposed consequence (Col. 3:25). We can shout "grace" or "prosperity doctrines" all day long, but God clearly laid out the guidelines in the New Testament, which reinforces this principle. This does not mean God will not decide to show an act of grace in times of self-imposed need, but it is not to be expected! What is to be expected are the parameters and pre-stated guidelines of the New Testament.

Most Christians would probably agree that going into most forms of debt is a sin. What has puzzled me over the years is why these same believers will turn around and borrow (go into debt) to pay off old debt. This is like a Christian saying that Christians should not be involved in lawsuits, but on the other hand, divorces (which is a lawsuit) his spouse or sues his workman's compensation insurance company for more cash. There are typically two times when we will see the character of a "Christian" come to the surface: when he is desperate for cash or when he has too much of it.

Let's look at more of the lies in which the Antichrist perpetrates our character.

LIE 7 – ONE HAS TO BORROW TO MAKE MONEY.

Now there is a financial principle that Satan loves! This is a fancy way of saying this: "You have to gamble in order to have financial gain." Yes, it is gambling and records show that 90+ percent of the corporate world does it. There is no question that borrowing during a time of inflation increases one's assets. But financial success is not measured by our assets; but by the freedom from greed, worry, and bondage.

Borrowing is gambling with God's sovereignty. Loans are based on the false notion that "everything will be better tomorrow; therefore, I will borrow against today." In reality, we are stealing from our tomorrow. Since God is not going to finance our debt (Prov. 13:13), we can be assured we are taking the resources from our tomorrow in order to survive for our today. God said He would care for us in our today. Our responsibility is to care for and preserve our tomorrows.

"Come now, you who say, 'Today or tomorrow we will go to such and such a city, and spend a year there and engage in business and make a profit.' Yet you do not know what your life will be like tomorrow. You are just a vapor that appears for a little while and then vanishes away" (James 4:13-14).

What if we quoted the opposite of this lie: "You have to become a slave to a lender if you are to make money." How stupid does that sound? Hmm...

"The rich rules over the poor, And the borrower becomes the lender's slave" (Prov. 22:7).

LIE 8 – BEING MY OWN BOSS IS MY LIFETIME GOAL

Those of us who have been to the top of this pile don't quote this anymore. This lie runs counter to the very nature of Jesus Christ's teachings, on both serving and being successful in life. Jesus was always preaching the mandate of last place. Those who shall be great shall be least, those in first place will be in last, serve those who persecute you, he who loves his life will lose it, and the list goes on from there. Jesus' goal for us, is not for us to become our own boss, but to be SERVANT UNTO ALL.

" 'But the greatest among you shall be your servant. Whoever exalts himself shall be humbled; and whoever humbles himself shall be exalted' " (Matt. 23:11-12).

I believe some of the greatest leaders in history have been those who mastered the act of serving the common folk. When our focus is on serving others, we may be lifted up and invited to serve in a leadership capacity;

but, the goal should always be to remain as a slave – first unto Christ and secondly unto man.

"For he who was called in the Lord while a slave, is the Lord's freedman; likewise he who was called while free, is Christ's slave" (1 Cor. 7:22).

LIE 9 – I HAVE THE RIGHT AND PRIVILEGE TO DECIDE HOW I SPEND MY MONEY; AFTER ALL, I'M THE ONE WHO EARNED IT

Seriously – let us see how this person reacts under unjust management or when someone doesn't pay him for what he earned. First of all, the one he is expecting payment from is not the final decision maker on the paycheck – God is. God can turn any leader to match His lessons assigned to His children, which includes withholding just payment for a just day's wages. Secondly, the money we "have earned" does not belong to us. We are only stewards of the allotted money. People who live out this lie are usually in the nasty habit of stealing from God's storehouse. Yes, those who demand their right to be paid because it is their money are usually the ones who are not consistent in their tithes (10% to the church) and offerings (10% to the needy). That is a grand total of 20% of our "money earned."

" 'Will a man rob God? Yet you are robbing Me! But you say, "How have we robbed You?" In tithes and offerings. You are cursed with a curse, for you are robbing Me, the whole nation of you! Bring the whole tithe into the storehouse, so that there may be food in My house, and test Me now in this,' says the LORD of hosts, 'if I will not open for you the windows of heaven and pour out for you a blessing until it overflows' " (Mal. 3:8-10).

LIE 10 – FINANCIAL SUCCESS MEANS OVERCOMING EVERY OBSTACLE THAT GETS IN THE WAY OF MY FINANCIAL GOALS

Hmmm – what if God is the one putting the obstacles in place? Shall a man be so determined to succeed at the cost of going against the hand of God? I wouldn't advise trying it. I have watched too many arrogant young men and women attempt this fruitless feat and find themselves sitting in a counselor's office begging for help. How easy it is for us to forget the ordinances of God:

"Turn to my reproof, behold, I will pour out my spirit on you; I will make my words known to you" (Prov. 1:23).

"The ransom of a man's life is his wealth, but the poor hears no rebuke" (Prov. 13:8).

Many times, obstacles are given to us by Him to reprove us. He designs these obstacles so we will turn from our own nasty ways and willingly follow His Divine and Holy pathway of truth and freedom.

Many times God has to fix a fix on us, to fix the fix of us always trying to fix ourselves or others. These obstacles could be holy and anointed by God.

LIE 11 – I CAN BUILD A SUCCESSFUL MINISTRY/BUSINESS WITH A WELL QUALIFIED ADVERTISEMENT PROGRAM

In the world of ministry, we call this "a black hole." The churches, as well as "Christian businesses," have thrown too much good money into this black hole. Since when does God need to be advertised? Don't get me wrong. There is nothing wrong with getting the word out for announcing times, dates, and topics of ministry/business activities; but to hire a firm to promote in order to profit – probably not. The old school workers will tell us there is nothing like the promotions of satisfied customers or word of mouth. The more honest and Christ-centered the "product," the less "advertising" is needed. There is no sin in advertising; it is in the motive behind the advertisement. The scriptural counsel is that we should not praise ourselves, but we should let others praise us instead.

"Let another praise you, and not your own mouth; A stranger, and not your own lips" (Prov. 27:2).

Have you ever thought what it is going to be like for the Christians, in the final years, who have lived off of the belief of "prosperity doctrines?" Prosperity doctrines only work in a working economy! They do not function in poverty nations or nations ruled by tyrants. The Antichrist will be a tyrant; in fact, he will make all other tyrants in history look like school yard bullies. I hate to say it, but America is soon to join the poverty nations of the world. Any nation or people who are in long-term debt are in poverty! They just act like they aren't.

What is a nation to do? "Go, sell the oil and pay your debt, and you and your sons can live on the rest" (2 Kings 4:7). The advice God offers a people is no different than to that of a nation. America's 13 trillion dollar debt would require every working American to donate (or tax) 50% of his income, for several generations, in order to be free from foreigners "calling in our debt." That will never happen, and if it did, there is NOT enough time to get the lenders off our nation's back. The simple fact is the nations that are debt free, in the final years, will be the toughest nations for the Antichrist to rule.

When parents are in debt, their children are in debt. Satan knows this principle to be true. This is why he places an entire family in debt, by stupid decisions parents make. The enemy knows God is glorified when children's needs are met. He also knows that parents who remain debt free, have children who are protected by God. Satan is not accustomed to accepting this without a fight, for he HATES selfless givers.

God is looking for parents to stand between heaven and earth, to distribute heaven's wealth everywhere! We are not talking about "cash." Rather, we are talking about the wealth of truth and principle. In this process, the "cash" aspect of the giver is oftentimes increased as a result of being willing to be the mediator of God's miraculous flow of economy.

"And God is able to make all grace abound to you, so that always having all sufficiency in everything, you may have abundance for every good deed" (2 Cor. 9:8).

Riches come from God and God alone. When a man thinks he can obtain or earn money to sustain himself on his own, he is soon to learn that by one decision of the government, an employer, or tragedy – it is all gone.

LIE 12 – WE CAN MEASURE OUR LEVEL OF SUCCESS BY THE AMOUNT OF MONEY WE OBTAIN OR EARN

Those who think money and success have something in common are vain and completely deceived. This is one of the toughest lessons for any Christian to learn.

"He who loves money will not be satisfied with money, nor he who loves abundance with its income. This too is vanity" (Eccl. 5:10).

Money does not satisfy the human soul! The false sense of success being equal with money will trap every person who is not secure in his identity in Christ – guaranteed.

People who live by this lie usually end up in divorce and bankruptcy courts. I cannot tell you how many people I have counseled over the years who were "millionaires" one week and asking for "handouts" the next. I even had one case where a man overworked his entire life in order to have the "nest egg." On his first retirement vacation, he had a fatal heart attack on the fifth hole of his first golf game.

This lie is based on the assumption that one's emotional needs (such as peace, security, happiness, acceptance, and fulfillment) will be met through the storage of money. Didn't anyone ever tell these people that "money has wings like birds?" Money never, and I mean never, supplies the satisfaction our soul searches for! Without having a secure identity in Christ, our financial decisions will be based upon plastic and metal. If we expect to gain from money what only God can provide, then money becomes our god.

"For the love of money is a root of all sorts of evil, and some by longing for it have wandered away from the faith and pierced themselves with many grief's" (1 Tim. 6:10).

LIE 13 – IF I REACH THE TOP OF THE SUCCESS PILE, I WILL BE SOMEBODY

Nothing smells more than the stench of a person crawling to the top of the pile of pride. Enviably crawling to the top means stepping on people to get there. People who buy into this lie oftentimes stink with pride and usually use godship terms like, "I'm proud of you." God told David exactly what He thinks about people doing this.

"But God is the Judge; He puts down one and exalts another" (Psalm 75:7).

Anyone who lifts himself up – God will not! In fact, if we take this verse for what the Hebrew actually is communicating, anyone who lifts himself up God will literally put him down. Ouch!!

Each and every person who believes he is responsible for his success will sooner, or later, experience the broken relationship with the ones who helped him reach it – and that includes God.

Out of the seven things God says He hates, pride is mentioned three times. Pride is nothing less than achieving what "I" want and when "I" want it, all the while living under the deception "I" did it alone. The truth of the matter is that whatever we achieve, God and others have done the achieving with, and most of the time, for us.

"There are six things which the LORD hates, yes, seven which are an abomination to Him: Haughty eyes, a lying tongue, and hands that shed innocent blood, a heart that devises wicked plans, feet that run rapidly to evil, a false witness who utters lies, and one who spreads strife among brothers" (Prov. 6:16-19).

The only hope we have as children of the King is that He is successful, without all of our efforts to make Him successful!

His ability is our inability and our inability is our assurance of Salvation. God is such a gracious Father, for He waits to glorify His abilities only when we come to the end of our own ridiculous attempts to glorify ourselves. He is a "pedestal kicker" more than all others. When we work tirelessly to put ourselves up on a pedestal, He is quick to kick that pedestal right out from underneath us. As soon as we cease to function in the power of human energy and tap into the unlimited resources of His world through Christ Jesus, we will have supernatural abilities to be successful as children of God -- even if it comes with the price tag of being labeled by the world as unsuccessful!

Lies, lies, and more lies. The enemy is ever so quick to make up a new one every time we get close to renouncing the last. What we all need is a fresh offering of discernment that acts like radar against the lies of the provocative evil one. Even though God does not, Satan is a god who changes with the times. The way he accomplishes changing the face of Christianity is through more lies.

LIE 14 – TO BE A SUCCESSFUL CHRISTIAN IN THE WORLD, WE MUST LEARN TO COMPROMISE

To compromise is to agree to give up a part of what we consider to be absolute truth for the sake of the argument, or to avoid rejecting another. To put it bluntly, it is an agreement to lie to one another. If we compromise basic issues in discussions, we will ultimately begin to compromise biblical truth for financial gain. Statistics prove that very few Christians choose NOT to compromise, when they are in the position of being able to advance in their careers. Most actually believe it is an active part of true honorable Christianity. One of my favorite preachers said it best:

"If we obey God it is going to cost other people more than it costs us, and that is where the sting comes in. If we are in love with our Lord, obedience does not cost us anything, it is a delight, but it costs those who do not love Him a good deal. If we obey God it will mean that other people's plans are upset, and they will jibe us with it - "You call this Christianity?" We can prevent the suffering; but if we are going to obey God, we must not prevent it, we must let the cost be paid.

Our human pride entrenches itself on this point, and we say - I will never accept anything from anyone. We shall have to, or disobey God. We have no right to expect to be in any other relation than our Lord Himself was in (Luke 8:2-3).

Stagnation in spiritual life comes when we say we will bear the whole thing ourselves. We cannot. We are so involved in the universal purposes of God that immediately we obey God, others are affected. Are we going to remain loyal in our obedience to God and go through the humiliation of refusing to be independent, or are we going to take the other line and say -

I will not cost other people suffering? We can disobey God if we choose, and it will bring immediate relief to the situation, but we shall be a grief to our Lord. Whereas if we obey God, He will look after those who have been pressed into the consequences of our obedience. We have simply to obey and to leave all consequences with Him.

"Beware of the inclination to dictate to God as to what you will allow to happen if you obey Him." –Oswald Chambers

True Christianity is costly. When we compromise, we are attempting to regulate God as to how much rejection He is permitted to sanction in our lives.

One of the most used excuses of control for Christians is how they make and spend their money. These "types" of Christians know there is a price for true Christianity and they simply are NOT willing to pay it. The price tag is usually rejection, isolation, and lack of promotions or advancements. Therefore, in order to get those "well deserved" promotions, they close their eyes to the principles of God by not reading their Bibles. In fact, my counseling experience with people of struggle like this is they rarely study the Word of God on any topic, let alone God's miraculous plan of economy.

God is the One who chooses to advance us in our professions/callings. There are many demonstrations of this in the Word. One of my favorites is the story of Joseph. He was a young man of integrity when his brothers tried to dispose of him by ultimately selling him as a slave. After Joseph was enslaved, he still maintained his integrity and lived in truth. Because of his reputation, God gave Him His favor and advanced him to be second in charge of all of Egypt. That kind of integrity and honor is rare in our society today.

Each of us must accept that God's standards of living are NOT to advance us, but to humble us into complete dependence on Him. Once this dependence is proven, we then are advanced in our faith – which oftentimes includes worldly advancements.

Compromise is for the deceived or weak. May we all be challenged by that statement!

LIE 15 – IN ORDER TO GET ANYWHERE IN THIS WORLD, WE BE MUST A MOVER AND SHAKER. IT'S NOT WHAT WE KNOW – IT'S WHO WE KNOW

Yeah, that might work if you're a bully! I don't mean to insult those who practice such ideologies, but people who live out this lie are acting as liars. How do I know this? I was guilty of this enough to be hung by my own string of names and influences that I self-propagated. I was so insecure as to who I was, I would use the names and positions of people I knew, or wished I knew, in order to stand taller in my little self-made world of pretend. The problem was when I actually got to know some of these "infamous" people, I became disappointed in them due to their level of shallowness. When I realized just how insecure they were, it only made things worse for me. Here I was investing all of my illusive projections into an image that was even shallower than my own pool of discontentment. In fact, in most cases, God ended up having me minister to them even though I was suffering as the "wannabe."

When another man lives off the reputation of another man, he only can advance as far as the length of that man's nose. In other words, we suffer God from truly being able to use His full potential in us to live out His true achievements. Attempting to gain love, acceptance, and favor from the rich and famous is not only condemned by God, it condemns God and puts our lives at risk!

"When you sit down to dine with a ruler, consider carefully what is before you, and put a knife to your throat if you are a man of great appetite. Do not desire his delicacies, for it is deceptive food. Do not weary yourself to gain wealth, Cease from your consideration of it. When you set your eyes on it, it is gone. For wealth certainly makes itself wings like an eagle that flies toward the heavens. Do not eat the bread of a selfish man, or desire his delicacies; for as he thinks within himself,

so he is. He says to you, 'Eat and drink!' But his heart is not with you. You will vomit up the morsel you have eaten, and waste your compliments" (Prov. 23:1-8).

Hmm – "Do not eat the bread of a selfish man or desire his delicacies." Well, there goes my "power lunches." I use to consider it quite odd that God would ask us not to eat with selfish people, but now that I understand the wisdom of identity – I get it. God said that for as he (a man) thinks of himself, so he is. Identity comes from what each person thinks of him or herself. The way to find out what a man thinks of himself is by how he eats and who he breaks bread with. Those who impress with "power lunches" are to be watched closely. Rarely are their hearts with us, but usually are out to further advance their own wealth.

Take it from someone who was a nobody, who became a somebody, then was reduced to being a nobody. Wealth and influence have wings; here today and gone the next.

LIE 16 – THERE IS NO TRUE HONOR IN BEING POOR OR IN SECOND PLACE

Really? Then Jesus was a rich carpenter who had a string of furniture franchises peppered throughout the Holy Land. Better yet, was He a liar when he said that it was best to be in last place?

"Sitting down, He called the twelve and said to them, 'If anyone wants to be first, he shall be last of all and servant of all' " (Mark 9:3).

OK, let's read this again. "If anyone wants to be first, he shall be last of all and servant of all." This might give us a window into the agenda of God as we watch "Christians" who have bought into these lies fall like autumn leaves from a tree. I have been humbled by God more times than I want to admit. It seems (or is) that every time I try to be in first place in anything, He is quick to place me at the end of the line. The more I work at being at the end of the "food line," the sooner I find myself talking to a "king."

Whether my poverty is a result of violating God's principles of economy, refusing to learn about God's character, withholding my tithes and offerings, or simply realizing my need for God – I am discovering God's control of circumstances is normal, natural, and neutral. Those who fight this truth fight God, the Author of the Universe. If stupid is as stupid does, then we all self-torment over stupidity. Big things often come in small packages. Since the world views Jesus as a poor poverty stricken nobody, I am strongly reconsidering being a SOMEBODY!

"For you know the grace of our Lord Jesus Christ, that though He was rich, yet for your sake He became poor, so that you through His poverty might become rich" (2 Cor. 8:9).

"For if anyone thinks he is something when he is nothing, he deceives himself" (Gal. 6:3).

CHAPTER 12

RECOGNIZING GOD'S CORRECTION

"Turn to my reproof, Behold, I will pour out my spirit on you; I will make my words known to you. Because I called and you refused, I stretched out my hand and no one paid attention; And you neglected all my counsel And did not want my reproof; I will also laugh at your calamity; I will mock when your dread comes, When your dread comes like a storm And your calamity comes like a whirlwind, When distress and anguish come upon you" (Prov. 1:23-27).

God's ways to riches is quite different than that of man. God says that if we simply, " 'Seek first His kingdom and His righteousness, and all these things will be added to you' " (Matt. 6:33). Man typically has a different approach to the "panic of need."

For those of you who are married, you know this to be true. When husbands overcome obstacles to get what they want: wives and children react poorly, investments go south, health problems evolve, all the get rich quick schemes fail, children rebel and act up, finances collapse, and their marriages and families go "belly up." Even if persistent self-will creates wealth, it quickly turns to a sorrowful wealth.

Ladies, did you know that most men make blundering financial decisions because of a destructive self-rejection cycle? It is completely true. Check out the chart below:

Male Manifestation	Woman's Response
1. **INFERIORITY:** When a man fails to accept his identity (or lack of it) in Christ, he develops deep feelings of "feeling less than others."	➢ **INSECURITY:** When a woman watches a man's inferiority, she loses her need to admire him and look to him for leadership – she becomes her own leader.

2. **BLING, BLING:** A man who typically does not accept himself as God does, tends to adorn his masculinity with "man toys" and symbols of status.

➢ **FEAR:** Being in the presence of a fearful woman is a terrifying thing. Women are designed by God to resist debt. She might outwardly accept it, but inwardly, she is going to the dogs.

3. **POOR PRIORITIES:** All men are motivated by having financial goals; it is a part of being a provider. Most men commit the sin of "putting the little woman to work" outside the home.

➢ **DIVIDED LOYALTY:** A woman is designed to be loyal to one leader at a time. When she is put in the position to serve two masters, sooner or later, she will choose one of those masters to give herself to.

4. **FEAR OF REJECTION:** Men, who expect their wives to help support the family, surrender part of their God-given responsibilities as providers. This will only make his "small man" syndrome worse. Soon, he will project his own self-identified rejection onto his wife and children.

➢ **RESENTMENT:** Women react to male self-rejection with feelings of resentment, *not* self-pity. The more a man "feels sorry for himself," the less she respects his manhood. This only furthers both of their desires to "look outside the home" for love, acceptance and forgiveness.

5. **JUMPING TO CONCLUSIONS:** Now that he has formed an independent spirit in his wife, he reacts by anger outbursts with massive attempts to gain control over his abandoned leadership.

➤ **SEPARATION:** Women hate being controlled by anger. The more he reacts with anger, the more she makes plans to separate herself from this anger-infested "mad man." Oftentimes, she feels abused.

I am not sure I understand why immorality almost always has a "kissing cousin" relationship with financial problems, but it is true. I have been counseling professionally for over 30 years and I cannot tell you how many times I have connected immorality to money. It would blow your mind if you could see what most counselors see in sessions. Due to this reality, I want to show you the five main manifestations of men who have financial problems and how their wives respond to them.

Male Manifestation	Woman's Response
LACK OF SELF-CONTROL: It is good that a man is "attached at the hip" to his wife physically, emotionally, and spiritually. If he is immoral with her before marriage, he gives her permission to …	➤ **SUFFER GUILT:** She lowers her standard to keep him showing her affection; but, her damaged self-respect starts a process of distrust and doubt that her husband can manage anything – let alone money.
SEX, SELF, & SENSUALITY: If a man starts the relationship with an "I have sexual needs" mentality, he soon becomes quick to ignore her sensual "hot spots." Sex then becomes all about him and his "needs."	➤ **FRIGID:** She begins seeing her husband as selfish and out for his own pleasure – she grows cold to touch. She often spends "his money" to fulfill her own pleasure "needs."

DEMANDS: He reacts to her frigid behavior and overspending, by demanding "payment" for her indulgent pleasures (spending) - by increasing his demands for more sex.

PROVING MASCULINITY: Men hate feeling like they are not man enough to please their wives. He reacts to her cold ways by proving his love through "guilt gifts" – more toys for her (more debt).

WORKAHOLIC: Since they both have more toys than they can afford, he must invest himself in work - every spare hour he can muster up. He spends less time with his wife and children and more time with "significant others."

➢ **MORE FRIGIDITY:** She now has the proof that he does not love her. She shuts herself off from him physically, emotionally, and spiritually. Oftentimes, she starts fantasizing about how other men might take care of her.

➢ **SHOPAHOLIC:** She responds to his "guilt gifts" with "bring it on." She now finds comfort and security in temporal things. This binds her to financial bondage and family destruction.

➢ **I'M OUT OF HERE:** She gives up on him meeting her needs through debt and begins turning her focus onto the idea of living without him. At first she lives with him "together separately" and then seriously contemplates an affair or divorce.

It is critical for men and women to recognize the signs and symptoms of being reproved by God for allowing debt. It took me three times of God completely freeing me from debt and walking right back into it, before I was able to recognize the signs of being reproved by God.

I hope and pray that it doesn't take that many times for you, or your loved ones, to learn such a valuable lesson. If it does, I must warn you dear reader, the road ahead of you will be painful and full of unbelievable challenges and testings (Rev. 3:10). If you pass these tests, you will be a better child of the living God.

CHAPTER 13

TEN SIGNS OF REPROOF

Being reproved by God is not a pleasant thing to be forced to embrace. In Job 37, we learn that whether for the sake of correction, for God to prove He is our God, or for the Divine purpose of love -- it is He -- who "causes it to happen." Knowing this, our eyes will hopefully look to Truth. Since God is the One who chooses to reprove us in His way and in His timing, we need to allow these circumstances to weaken us, instead of taking on these afflictions like they are some kind of challenge. If we don't fall to our knees in weakness and brokenness, our hearts will turn harder than a heart attack. Why? Because we have refused to REPENT and allow God to change our ways.

Allow me to offer to you the ten most obvious signs of reproof:

1. **Being in situations where we "think" we have to borrow money in order to survive**: God knows that we are not to turn those away who come to us to borrow. But in the same breath, He tells us not to borrow. What this means is that God understands the way poverty-stricken people think. He also knows they will come to us for help by way of "short-term debts." It does NOT mean that God places approval on short or long-term debts. What it does mean is that He does not want us to turn away from those people who "think" they need to borrow to survive. When we are the poverty-stricken ones in need, with the big boat in the garage, He knows a reproof is in line.
2. **Overdue bills:** There are two types of overdue bills. The first is the most innocent; those who have bills due that are not a result of debt spending (like rent, utilities, etc.). The second kind of "overdue bills" is a result of debt mentality. With those kinds of overdue bills, God is not quick to send a "miraculous provider" to bail us out. He can, but He usually allows the debt to become our tutor to quicken our hearts to detest additional debt.

3. **Grandiose thinking:** Proverbs 28:22 says: "A man with an evil eye hastens after wealth and does not know that want will come upon him." A tall tale sign that we are about to be reproved by God is that we are suffering with a mind running after wealth. If we want to challenge the hand of God, just set our eyes upon being wealthy and we will quickly see the other side of God's hand. It doesn't matter if the Christian is emergent (God doesn't want me unhappy) in his thinking, this WILL provoke the hand of God.
4. **Insomnia:** Have you ever noticed how well you sleep when you have earned the bread on your table? I sure have – it feels great. Solomon was a very wise man, BUT he didn't always work for a living. Most of it was handed to him on a silver tray. After too many years of this kind of "want not," he came to this conclusion: "The sleep of the working man is pleasant, whether he eats little or much; but the full stomach of the rich man does not allow him to sleep" (Eccl. 5:12). I have a feeling Solomon had a bunch of sleepless nights.
5. **Unexpected and planned losses:** Those who look for much, oftentimes end up with little. Have you ever worked tirelessly for something and in just a few short moments, it's gone – blown into the wind? My counseling career is filled with such stories; people who just can't figure out why God would take away all that a man has spent his life working for. I have the unfortunate experience of helping them embrace the truth of Haggai 1:9: " 'You look for much, but behold, it comes to little; when you bring it home, I blow it away. Why?' declares the LORD of hosts, 'Because of My house which lies desolate, while each of you runs to his own house.' " Anytime man puts an emphasis on taking care of his own house before the house of God, well – he had better "buckle up" - the wind is about to blow.
6. **Can't enjoy what we have:** When we are on the side of the fence that has brown grass, at least we think, it is easy to judge the ones on the "greener" side as having no excuse to "enjoy all of life." The truth being, most wealthy people don't enjoy what they have because they are always looking to more of what they don't have,

or an upgrade of what they do. This is a trap of Satan himself. This trap is so deceptive, most will create more debt to maintain this vicious cycle of doom. I say, let them have the green grass; it's usually artificial turf anyway. Being content with what we have, or don't have, is the key to turning the soil on our side of the fence to create a true produce of Life - a life that will sustain itself in the harshest times of affliction. This all starts by being content with our present wages! "And he said to them, 'Do not take money from anyone by force, or accuse anyone falsely, and be content with your wages' " (Luke 3:14).

7. **Being spiritually empty:** Any soul who cares for the world and it's riches more than replenishing his heart with the Word, will choke off the Word of God in his life and actually become unfruitful in all his ways (Matt. 13:22). A sad state of a man is when I am sharing the power of God's Word with him and the whole time, he has a look in his eyes like he didn't hear a word I was saying. Immediately after this Holy Spirit moment, he brings up something completely worldly. Hmm – dry bones.

8. **Suffering from unnecessary family pressure:** He that is greedy for more gain, money, influence, or power brings hardship and trouble upon his own house (Prov. 15:27). This is true in almost every financial bondage case I have ever assisted. Families are the first to go when a greedy heart demands to be filled. Women react to these "heads of home" by forsaking the home for that "special someone" who will "listen to them." All the while, these "heads of home" are gaining affection from women who are desperate for affection. Yes, my dear reader, money and immorality do go together.

9. **Money strikes back like the head of a snake:** Money has a funny way of paying for more than the bills. If we have too little of it, it will stress us to the point of physical exhaustion in finding ways to get it. If we have too much of it, we stress over worrying about how we're going to keep it. Money and health problems go hand in hand. Ecclesiastes 5:13 says: "There is a grievous evil which I have seen under the sun: riches being hoarded by their owner to his hurt." It is no wonder the most significant principle of God's

miraculous plan of economy is keeping the flow of money moving. Scriptures show us that if it stands still too long, it will devour us.
10. **Legal problems:** Have you ever met someone who has money, or strives tirelessly to get it, who DOESN'T have legal problems? I know of very few. Most money hungry people are either suing someone for more cash or are being sued, because they have too much of it.

"So if you have law courts dealing with matters of this life, do you appoint them as judges who are of no account in the church? I say this to your shame. Is it so, that there is not among you one wise man who will be able to decide between his brethren, but brother goes to law with brother, and that before unbelievers? Actually, then, it is already a defeat for you, that you have lawsuits with one another. Why not rather be wronged? Why not rather be defrauded? On the contrary, you yourselves wrong and defraud. You do this even to your brethren" (1 Cor. 6:4-8).

Each of us needs to stand on the shores of REALITY, face the pain, and accept the discipline of the Lord. People tend to make the word "reproof" more than what it is. Reproof from the Hebrew is a simple word picture, which is "re-proof" (revisiting the proof of truth until it is embraced). That is the goal, objective, and purpose of God allowing the ten most obvious signs of reproof.

CHAPTER 14
A NATION THAT OBEYS MONEY

The reason the world is in such bondage is debt. The only people who are at true peace with themselves are those who have no debt. The same concept works for the globalization of the world economy. The countries that have no debt will be the decision makers in the end-times. In fact, the lending countries will be the real "players" in the global empire of one world government, while holding the countries that owe them money in financial bondage.

If you're like most, you have heard the numbers being thrown around regarding the amount of debt the United States is in? According to a report by the *New York Times* in 2010, our national debt is about $12 trillion. The truth of the matter is this $12 trillion is only the "visible debt" the government wants you and me to see. Just to see a snapshot of the real picture, let's do a quick calculation of the real numbers:

Keep in mind that these numbers are dated back from 2009. Allow me to quote Dr. David Jeremiah:

"Fiscal economists use a term that designates the cause and magnitude of our debt: infinite horizon discounted value. While this term represents a highly complicated formula that determines the value of all promised benefits, current and future, in terms of our presenting day dollars going forward into the infinite future, its simple meaning is: the gap between promised Social Security and Medicare benefits accruing to every American with a registered Social Security number and the actual income from taxes in a given year. It is an approximation based on life expectancy in actuarials. For Social Security alone that gap is $17.5 trillion!

Unfortunately, Social Security is not our greatest problem. Medicare is many times worse. Our current Medicare program has three separate centers of coverage and funding. Medicare Part A covers hospital stays. Medicare Bart B covers doctor visits. The most recent addition to the Medicare programs, Part D, which covers prescriptions, took effect in 2006.

The current unfunded liability for Medicare Part A is $36.7 trillion; for Part B it is $37 trillion; and for Part D it is $15.6 trillion. The total liability of all three unfunded Medicare programs is $89.3 trillion. This is five times as much as the unfunded Social Security bill."

Now let's calculate some of these numbers. If we add the unfunded liability of all three parts of Medicare to the already unfunded liability of our Social Security, we will arrive at the mind-bending amount of $106.8 trillion. Wait, we are not done. Now, add our national debt of $12 trillion and that gives us the mind-altering total of $118.8 trillion. If we were to distribute that debt to all taxpaying citizens, each of us would be responsible for $383,000 or $1,532,000 per family of four. Those are the numbers of 2009. A June 2010 report says that another $1.4 trillion can be added to the 2009 debt and yet another $100 billion since January 1st of 2011. That is a grant total of $120.2 trillion dollars of actual debt.

In 2009, the interest on just the first $12 trillion alone (which we have to pay), was $383 billion. To help us put this into perspective, just to pay the interest on our national debt, the government took 40 cents from every dollar that came in from taxes. I hope it sank in what I just wrote – that is 40% of every American taxpayer just to stay above these eight countries calling in their debt!

Did you know that in 2009, 50% of our nation's public debt (that means *our* debt) is owned by foreign governments and financial institutions, like global banks? It is true. Here is a list of the top eight countries that hold the U.S. in debt:

China	$798.9 billion
Japan	$746.5 billion
United Kingdom	$230.7 billion
Muslim oil countries	$188.4 billion
Caribbean bankers	$169.3 billion
Brazil	$156.2 billion
Hong Kong	$142.0 billion
Russia*	$122.5 billion

*Russia became so angered by President Reagan's "star wars" and "Reaganomics" that they decided to work to put the U.S. into debt to their own country; just like Japan did after the U.S. did their checkmate, post-World War II. As you can see, Japan is now the lending master. In 2007, Russia owned no U.S. debt and now she is on the grand master list.

Here is a mind-bending factor: the U.S. is in so much debt that we are racking up an accursed amount of interest of $41 million per hour. To even make it more real: that's $984 million per day; $690,000 a minute; and $11,500 per second. If the government was to pay the interest and principle on our nation's debt, they would have to raise the taxes to 70 cents per dollar, increase the population by 400% and even then, it would take 7 generations to pay – that is assuming the United States government would *never* go into debt AGAIN. With the abortion and euthanasia rate tripling each year, this simply will never happen! It has already been determined that the countries, or religions, that defy divorce, abortion, euthanasia, and debt will rule in the end. The sobering reality is – the United States of America will not be one of them. We are too far gone. Am I being a defeatist? No – a realist! So, what is to happen to our country?

Since the odds of America honoring biblical guidelines when it comes to spending money is next to nil, we have to consider the proposed idea of the European Common Wealth Commission and the G20 - turn America the Republic over to Europe. Some say this will never happen. Really? Since when does the slave tell the lender what to do? If Americans are still so arrogant to think we are the "most powerful country in the world," we deserve to be humbled in such a fashion. Let's take a look at what common sense commentator, Charles Goyette says:

"America's debts at any level -$12 trillion…won't be paid. They will simply be rolled over again and again until America's creditors are unwilling to loan any longer. The nation is in the same position as someone who has taken a cash advance from his Visa card to meet his mortgage payment, and then has taken out a new MasterCard credit line to pay his Visa bill. Credit card debt juggling may appear to work in the short run, but it is a road to financial ruin. And just as compound interest is said to be the investor's best friend, it is the debtor's worst nightmare, as debt growth becomes exponential."

What is a nation to do? As with personal debt, cut up the credit cards and decide NEVER to go into debt again. Next, develop a plan that will ultimately get itself out of debt and stick to it. Finally, start selling off everything in the nation that is NOT a necessity. Commit to giving 50% of the sale profits to national debt; 40% to internal debt; and 10% to caring for the needy, by starting with the elderly. Is this plan too simple for a complex nation? Here is what God has to say about it:

"The law of the LORD is perfect, restoring the soul; the testimony of the LORD is sure, making wise the simple" (Psalm 19:7).

"The LORD preserves the simple; I was brought low, and He saved me" (Psalm 116:6).

"The unfolding of Your words gives light; it gives understanding to the simple" (Psalm 119:130).

God's ways are absolute and perfect. When an individual or a nation obeys them, the person, or nation, is restored. The only tangible way to make this a real possibility is to humble the self-proclaimed "wise men" to simplicity. Without functioning simply, we will not be preserved by the Lord. Those who are not preserved by Him erode and are turned over to the consequences of their wrong (Col. 3:25).

CHAPTER 15

CHOOSE THIS DAY

The Word is clear; we cannot serve two masters at one time. The person will ultimately hate the one and love the other, or minimally, will cling to one and reject the other. In fact, God goes on to say that it is impossible to serve God and money at the same time (Matt. 6:24).

God wants us to choose today which one we will serve. Here are ten fleshly decisions that men, women, and nations make that put them in a position of being humbled by the Lord:

1. **Using Christianity to Gain Personally:** People, or nations, who refer to themselves as "Christian" but yet, follow the mandates and principles of an evil world that mocks God. God is not to be mocked. In fact, if He is mocked in this fashion, He is obligated by Himself to effect "for whatever a man (nation) sows this he will also reap" (parentheses mine, Gal. 6:7; also see Num. 22-24; Jude 11; Rev. 2:14).

2. **Playing with the Edge of Evil:** Playing with the edge of evil is using demonic and worldly answers to bail yourself out of the consequences granted by God. A good example of this is when Lot (Abraham's nephew) separated himself from his patriarch (Abraham) and chose to submit himself to the land of Sodom, a land that was known for being lush and green with prosperity. Lot began swinging deals with the leaders of Sodom, thinking that he would be an influence on them. Well, we know how that story turned out. God not only turned Lot's wife into a pillar of salt, but after blasting the twin cities of Sodom and Gomorrah, He turned the refreshing waters of the Dead Sea to salt. Now the land has a difficult time even producing weeds (Gen. 12-14).

3. **Mixing True Faith with Selfish Flesh:** The obvious result of this is no more "true faith." For those who want to go Emergent/Lukewarm, do this. People who mix principles of God

with lies of Satan get the worst of the worst treatment from God. Not only does Satan love this, he finds in this, error globalization. On one hand, the "believer" says he believes in God, but he uses the ways of the enemy to practice life. He takes a perfectly good principle and turns it into a God tolerating sin – like the postmodern "Christian" view of abortion and divorce. You want to wrestle with an angel, do this (Gen. 27-34).

4. **Submitting Yourself to Jealousy:** The evidence of being filled with jealousy is contradicting a teacher of Truth (Acts 13:45). The crazy thing is that contradiction almost always turns into blasphemy of God. When a person comes against a Truth preacher of the Word, he comes against God. I often refer to it as "intellectual competition." Most humans buy into the lie of "intellectual rights" or individual self-conceived thought, which means the human thinks he has some type ownership of thought. It is all based in jealousy! Every thought I think or word I write is either from the mind of Christ or from my flesh, which is the receiver (antenna) of Satan. This is why our flesh must lay in the ground when we die. The "Christian" world has gone so far out on a limb with this lie that churches terminate or destroy the reputations of godly men and women who use words of God in other communicators without "permission." People who think they have intellectual rights are a people who think they are God (Josh. 7).

5. **Using Christianity Commercially:** There is no better story in my eyes than of Gideon. Most are familiar with his miraculous work of conquering the Midianites to free Israel. Few are aware of the offer placed before Gideon, by the people, to be their king. He refused and asked instead for all the gold earrings of the enemy. He then took this gold and made a gold ephod (vest) for the priest to wear, much like the story of Aaron's golden calf. The vest became an object of worship. Gideon then took on many wives and had seventy sons. After he died, God judged his entire family. (You can read the gory details in Judges 8). This mixture of true belief and commercialism tossed a nation to the enemy for many generations.

6. **Taking the Credit for God's Work:** I have an idea. Let's take God's thoughts, Words, and inspirations through the power of the Holy Spirit; copyright them; and then require mankind to pay for them – with the promise to never rewrite, reprint, reproduce, or digitally master them. Yes, I'm being facetious! Who, in God's name, came up with copyright anyway? This has stopped the multiplicity of the Gospel more than any other form of commercialism. Original thought is God. Enough said (see 2 Kings 5).

7. **Worshipping Jesus and Money:** This is the bling-bling rich young ruler that Jesus was addressing in Luke 18:18-34. I am not sure how true indwelt Christians can turn their poor poverty stricken Savior into a "Prosperity Doctrine" teacher? It has always been a mystery to me. Smart moneymakers have always found it easy to package and expect all others to be able to do what they do, which is why they are rich. If I had a dollar (Did I just say that?) for every time I heard some moneymaker say, "If I could do it, you certainly can." Prosperity Doctrines are nothing more, or less, than multileveling Jesus. They cut and paste Scriptures in order to maintain their service to two masters, much like the rich young leader. This leader showed quick and responsible actions, came to Jesus, and appeared to have an ability to be taught. But once the real challenge was put before him, he ran into the arms of his real master – money. Why did Jesus ask him to "Sell everything he had and give it to the poor" as a test of his inquest? (verse 22). It wasn't just to test the motive to his question, but Jesus was also practically checking to see if he would fulfill one of the leading obligations of a new believer.

"For there was not a needy person among them, for all who were owners of land or houses would sell them and bring the proceeds of the sales and lay them at the apostles' feet, and they would be distributed to each as any had need" (Acts 4:34-35).

8. **Rating Out Another Christian:** The first sign of love is loyalty! Today, we live in a society of children rising up against their

patriarchs and even killing them. In the final hours of the end-times, we will find parents turning their own Christian children over to the guardians of the Antichrist for destruction. Why? For the love of money. A man's loyalty is where his money is invested. As many of you know, Judas was the "coin keeper" for the disciples – that would be the banker for you and me. It was his responsibility to carefully manage the money in order to move the ministry from town to town. Remember his response to Jesus having his feet washed by Mary? He was upset because she was using expensive perfume that could be sold in the marketplace for 300 pence and given to the poor. I'm not sure Judas was really interested in feeding the poor; I do think he was controlled by people, places, and things that had value. How do we now this? He ultimately sold his Savior for 30 pieces of silver. Would Judas have sold his own grandma? Of course he would have. After all, he sold his own soul to Satan. Jesus called him the devil, meaning he became possessed or owned (Matt. 26-27).

9. **Buying Praise:** One time I was drinking a Pepsi drink as I was waiting to pick up one of my kids at the local Christian school (before our homeschool years). A financial supporter was observing me without me knowing it. He walked over to my car and said, "So that's how you spend my money." Needless to say, I wrote him a letter the following day and encouraged him to stop supporting our ministry. Many "Christians" financially support their churches, favorite causes, or charity for the pure (maybe not so pure) need for praise. Let's face it; givers get high praise and usually get specialized treatment for doing so. This kind of praise and admiration is more costly than the donation – it enslaves the ministry to the giver. I have turned thousands of dollars away due to God revealing to me the motive. It is like stealing from the offering plate. I know I will offend some with what I am about to write; but, all tax-deductible donations are subtle acts of Ananias and Sapphira (Acts 5). We have been "duped" into giving, in order to get our giving back through our tax returns. Don't get me wrong. I, too, use the 501c3 status to help givers gain this

advantage. But, the real hardcore truth of the matter is the "right hand should not see what the left hand is giving."

10. **Buying Spirituality:** A few years ago, I had a counselee slide a check in front of me after a particular session. I looked down at the check and it was written to me to the tune of $10,000. After asking him what the money was for, he said "Take care of your family." I looked at the check one more time and said, "Yes, Lord" in my head. I proceeded to slide the check back in front of him and I said, "From here on out, the counseling for you and your family is without the talk of money." Two years later, he was put in prison for using the same techniques in the business world. It is not uncommon for postmodern "Christians" to make offers like this. OK, maybe not as blatantly as my client, but certainly by rubbing shoulders with people who are more "spiritual" than they. People have the nasty habit of thinking their money, particularly donations, give them special privileges in spiritual places (Acts 8:9-24).

I think it is time for us to carefully review how we can truly serve God instead of money! If asked, most self-proclaimed Christians would say that they serve God rather than Satan. They would be quick to deny they love money more than Jesus. But when put to the test, most of these Christians would choose the quiet deceptions of money over true Christianity. How do I know this? When I ask, "If God asked you to sell everything you had, live in poverty the rest of your life, and beg for bread for the sake of the Gospel, would you do it? Most say, "Yes" – but leave my office maintaining their present lifestyle of debt.

CHAPTER 16

SERVING GOD OVER MONEY

Have you ever thought about the irony of someone asking if you would give up everything to serve Jesus? I certainly have. If we say "yes," we know God will soon test our motives. If we say "no," God will most likely bring us to the point of saying "yes." What is a Christian to do? Well, honestly, most Christians become lukewarm.

I can't change the fact that God tests whom He loves (Prov. 17:3). This is a real hardcore fact that we simply cannot escape if we love the Lord. Testing is a part of growth and growth is needed to sustain the attacks of the enemy. There are two primary principles I have found in the Scriptures that God requires of us, in order to get to the point of serving God rather than money.

ONE - List All the Things that You Love: What we love is what we worship. This practical principle drives you and me every day and moment of life. God will always go after the things that we love more than Him. It doesn't mean He will kill and destroy each of our huggable lovables. What it does mean is that He will direct us to bring the people, places, and things that summon our affections before the altar of sacrifice. If we cannot say with our actions that these objects of love are dedicated to Him, there is a serious problem with our walk in and with Him. He knows these objects WILL become objects of worship. When we start hugging a tree more than Jesus Christ, well, we are begging to be hung on it (Gal. 2:20).

The best way to find out if something is more important to you than God is by thinking, "If God took it away, would I go into a meltdown to the point of questioning God?" It could be one or more of any of the following: money, location, children, parents, job, church, ministry, material possessions, family heirlooms, or a host of others people, places, or things.

One of the most popular stories in the Bible that God uses to communicate the importance of this message is that of Abraham and his son Isaac (Gen. 21-22). Keep in mind, Abraham had to wait on God for 80+ years to get his son. God is now asking him to "offer him there for a burnt offering upon one of the mountains which I will tell you" (Gen. 22:2). God was testing Abraham of his loyalty to Him versus his son. God was also demonstrating the perfect kind of love: sacrificing the people, place, and things that mean the most to us, for the simple sake of love and loyalty to the One who created the things we hold on to the most. Plus, this was a prophetic act and replica of what God Himself was about to do with His own Son in the future.

Even though it appears that God is a "drama king" here, He isn't. God knows we tend to remember His principles longer when He places these memory markers, which usually come through painful sacrifices.

Just as with Abraham, we need to get alone with God and build our altar (on our knees on the side of our bed). List out our "gods" and ready ourselves to confess them before the living God as idols. Pray through the list in full honesty, claim God's forgiveness for our idolatry, and let Him know we are releasing these people, places, and things to death OR life, and that we will live with His choices regarding each of these items.

If you're not as confident with God as Abraham was regarding God's ability to raise his son from the dead, to fulfill the other promises He had given to Abraham, then ask God for that confidence. God never changes His promises to us because of our rebellion. If He said He would do something for or with us, He will; but He might require of us to sacrifice all that will get in the way of pure service. There is one thing for certain; whatever we give to God, He is able to protect and multiply far more than we.

"For this reason I also suffer these things, but I am not ashamed; for I know whom I have believed and I am convinced that He is able to guard what I have entrusted to Him until that day" (2 Tim. 1:12).

When we give up our most treasured items before the Lord, it activates His protective nature of those very things. We must continue to pray, "From this moment on, these things belong to You. I give them to You. I release my own rights over them and join You in your prerogative to manage them as You desire." If we ever stray from this point of prayer, He will start the testing all over again. It is like Abraham taking his knife and "stretching forth his hand" to slay his beloved son (Gen. 22:10).

Abraham could not get to the point of sacrificing his own son until he was willing to die to the human emotion he had for the earthly object of devotion. The action of dedicating his most beloved possession to the Lord was not complete until he did this. You and I must do the same thing and be willing to be thankful ahead of time for whatever He decides to do with our "letting go." I won't lie to you; there are times when He does, for His own reasons, take the object of worship away from us. But I believe, most of the time, He restores the items with a new sense of worship unto Him.

Just remember: God shares His glory with no one!

TWO - Plan on God Revealing His SUPERNATURAL Power: Abraham did not have to wait too long for God to show Himself. As soon as He was assured He had Abraham's heart and loyalty, He provided a different sacrifice. Abraham learned some very powerful lessons that day. He certainly learned that authentic sacrifice takes place in the core of a man's soul, not in the superficial act of self-sacrifice.

He also showed us that once we let go of the emotion connected with the object of worship, God will be able to show His wonderful miraculous power through the very people, places, and things that we held onto so tightly. Usually, they become the foundational building blocks of our ministry of service unto Him. In Abraham's case, even though God required him to sacrifice his son, God used the life of Isaac to continue building a great nation (Israel) through Abraham's seed. My encouragement to you is to make that list. Give Him your marriage, children, grandchildren, job, friendships, church, reputation, or whatever it is that toots your horn, AND lay it at the altar. Consider praying this prayer:

Lord Jesus Christ, I desire to walk after the Spirit and serve you in my daily living. I recognize that the sin of idolatry is a direct assault against Your divine nature. I acknowledge before You that the act of _____ is idolatry and sin. If this sin has been passed down to me through my ancestors, I break its power of influence through the blood of Jesus Christ. I accept Your redemption and forgiveness through the work of the cross. I recognize that it is only Your Son, through the indwelling Holy Spirit, who has the power to cause me to serve You and You alone. I choose to give You all the honor and glory that You deserve. I ask that the Holy Spirit bring the work of the crucifixion and resurrection of Jesus into the areas of my life, which these idols have consumed. Enable me to respond to Your prompting and voice to keep my eyes fixed on Jesus. Remind me that I am not to give divine attention to any person, place, or thing, including myself. Today, I entrust my victory over these idols completely into the hands of the Holy Spirit, as I choose to let Him take full control of me. It is in the blessed name of Jesus Christ I pray. Amen.

CHAPTER 17

ESTABLISH A PLAN OF GIVING

Can you imagine for one moment what it would be like to personally rob something from God? I mean, think about it; attempting to rob from a Being who knows all, sees all, and manages all. How stupid is that? It doesn't matter how stupid it is. It is done all day, every day, and by some of the most respected Christians in the world.

One of my favorite passages in the entire Bible is Malachi 3:8-10:

" 'Will a man rob God? Yet you are robbing Me! But you say, "How have we robbed You?" In tithes and offerings. You are cursed with a curse, for you are robbing Me, the whole nation of you! Bring the whole tithe into the storehouse, so that there may be food in My house, and test Me now in this,' says the LORD of hosts, 'if I will not open for you the windows of heaven and pour out for you a blessing until it overflows' " (Mal. 3:8-10).

Managing money and salvation through Christ Jesus go hand in hand. Does this sound a bit odd? Allow me to explain by asking you a series of questions:

ONE: What is the difference between tithes and offerings?

A tithing is completely different than an offering! A tithe is the first 10% of not only one's income, but also of every blessing that comes his way: food, clothing, money, drink, candy – you get the point. Even though 100% of what one earns or is given belongs to the Lord, the 10% is the portion that goes directly to the continuation of the Lord's work: church, ministries, etc. Tithing was an Old Testament requirement. Offerings were added in New Testament times as sacrificial giving, which was in no way to replace tithes to the Lord. Offerings are meant to be the giving portions, which are above and beyond the 10% required of the Lord. These offerings usually go to special needs, i.e. helping a neighbor, giving to the homeless, etc. (2 Cor. 9:6-8).

TWO: Is the Lord's tithe still to be a part of our lives today?

Yes. Tithing was established before God gave the law to Moses (Gen. 14:20). It has always been the Lord's way of guaranteeing resources for His earthly work. We learn in the book of Matthew that Christ continues to promote this requirement in the New Testament.

" *'Woe to you, scribes and Pharisees, hypocrites! For you tithe mint and dill and cummin, and have neglected the weightier provisions of the law: justice and mercy and faithfulness; but these are the things you should have done without neglecting the others'* " (Matt. 23:23).

Jesus not only supports the principle of tithing in this passage, but moves and challenges them to care for others through offerings.

THREE: What is the biblical reason for tithe?

As previously mentioned, tithes are needed for the vital support of the church worldwide, not just in our local communities. It not only keeps the church nourished, but it also puts us in the position of fearing God. Since the fear of God is the beginning of the knowledge of God (Ps. 1), we need to carefully review what develops fear in the believer.

"You shall surely tithe all the produce from what you sow, which comes out of the field every year. You shall eat in the presence of the LORD your God, at the place where He chooses to establish His name, the tithe of your grain, your new wine, your oil, and the firstborn of your herd and your flock, so that you may learn to fear the LORD your God always" (Deut. 14:22-23).

The reason why the church has gone emergent/lukewarm is because of the lack of respect and fear of God! Tithing is not about money – it is so much more than giving up a few bucks out of one's wallet. It is for the sole purpose of a relationship with God.

FOUR: Where should our tithe be given?

We can and should start with the Lord's local work (church). Is it wrong for us to save a portion of the 10% to go to the Church (Body of Christ) in other parts of the world? Not at all; in fact, it is a good practice. Our 10%

is for the function and development of the Body of Christ. We should always care for the church, ministries, and individuals who care for us and our household first. This is why my wife and I use our "offerings" to give above and beyond the Lord's local work. Here is how we prioritize our giving of offerings: feed our household, feed our needy neighbors, give to the surrounding communities, donate to national ministries, and then give "unto the world."

FIVE: When should we pay our tithe?

We should pay our tithe, or at least set it aside, directly after we are paid or given a blessing. Most get in the habit of using the first day of every week, which is not only a good idea, it is biblical.

"On the first day of every week each one of you is to put aside and save, as he may prosper, so that no collections be made when I come" (1 Cor. 16:2).

SIX: Does tithing include our time?

Yes. We are asked, if not required, to give of our first fruits – no matter what the fruit is. Time, or volunteering, is one of the most valuable tithes and offerings one can give. Don't fall into the mentality of paying your tithe to the church so the pastor can do the work. This is a great way to burn him out. God wants us to honor Him with every form of substance life has to offer us.

"Honor the LORD from your wealth and from the first of all your produce; so your barns will be filled with plenty and your vats will overflow with new wine" (Prov. 3:9-10).

SEVEN: What if I am in debt?

It doesn't matter if we are in debt, or not. In fact, it matters more. Someone who is in debt is considered to be a poor steward by the Lord. People who are in debt are usually in debt because they are in a nasty habit of robbing from God by not tithing. Whenever I am working with someone to get him out of debt, I immediately have him start tithing in order to open the floodgates of God's blessings and the power to deliver him from the debt. People with debt mentality are typically selfish people. Thus, they stop reaching out to help others because they are in a constant influx of their own perceived needs. It is a trap and this is why tithing is very important for those who are enslaved to lenders.

EIGHT: Should a wife tithe if her husband does not want her to?

Yes, but not with money! She can give her time, labor, and certain material blessings that her husband approves. Most selfish men, who don't want their wives to tithe, typically don't care if their wives give; they just don't want their wives giving their "hard earned cash" (Acts 9:36-43).

NINE: Should a husband tithe if his wife does not want him to?

Yes, but with a great deal of respect! Even if 87% of the American families do not support the fact that the man is the head of the home, it doesn't change the truth of God's Word. Men should not use this truth as a whip, but rather as a guiding tool to lead their wife and children to join him where he believes God is at work. It also needs to be noted that in cases of an unequally yoked marriage (one saved, one not), the head of the home should never give his tithe to charities that do not have the mission of leading the receiver to Christ or to a closer walk with Him.

TEN: What about back tithe I have not paid?

This is a decision that will have to be made between you and God. I have had clients who have gone back and calculated an estimate from their first job as a teenager, to those who start fresh from the day of discovery. Personally, I believe it is an issue of clear conscience before God. If He believes it is important to clear the conscious – then so be it. Keep in mind that not tithing is robbing God. Stealing is something most biblical counselors believe needs to be paid back. Whatever way you believe God is leading you, be cheerful while you do it (2 Cor. 9:6).

ELEVEN: Should we tithe on our gross or net income?

We should tithe on what comes into the net – not on what is left after the government takes out its portion of the fish. What is in the net is our first catch – first fruit.

TWELVE: Should I tithe on "dirty money?"

No! God doesn't want any part of man's dirty money. This would include netted income from: gambling, drug dealing, pornography sales, or any other ill-gotten gain. That is why I pushed that $10,000 check right back in front of the man who was buying my spirituality.

I had another case of ministering to the "number two" Mafia man in a given territory. After a year of difficult counseling, he got saved. His life completely changed and he was very grateful for the work of God through me. One day I was finishing up counseling and the front desk person said I had a client outside who needed to see me. I went out and to my surprise, there was a brand new Mercedes Coupe sitting there. He said, "It's yours." Even though his heart was pure, I graciously turned him down. One week later, he drove me out to one of his many building projects and asked me which four story model I liked best. For the fun of it, I told him the one I liked, not knowing what was coming next. He said, "It's yours." I asked him if this project was left over money from his Mafia days and he said, "Yes." I had the unpleasant experience of challenging him with separating himself from every investment and project that had "dirty money" connected to it – and he did!

THIRTEEN: Should a person tithe when the money is a tithe gift?

Yes, because that is God's miraculous plan of economy. If every first fruit was tithed, there would be no need for Medicaid, Medicare, Social Security, or insurance. There has always been plenty of money and resources to care for the wealthy, moderately wealthy, poor, and physically and mentally challenged. Plenty! The reason why we "need" these programs is because of all the wealth and poor stealing from God's simple 10%.

FOURTEEN: Can a tithe be used to pay for things spiritual?

Sure, if the item purchased is for the benefit of another. Typically, we need to avoid using God's purposed money to personally gain from it. I really don't think God makes a big deal about using tithe money to purchase a

Bible or other items that will benefit our growth, but it is NOT a good habit to get into.

FIFTEEN: Should I fear consequences if I decide not to tithe?

Absolutely! Robbing God from His storehouse is a serious offense to Him and His church. When we steal from God, we turn His hand of blessing away from us and move God to bring consequences for our wrong (Mal. 3:8-11; Col. 3:25).

SIXTEEN: Is it appropriate to involve my children in tithing?

Most certainly – children should be taught as early as they understand the value of material possessions and money. For example: when a child is given a candy bar, he should be taught to break off a 10th of it and give it to another (brother, sister, friend, etc.). It is important that we teach our children the practical principles of giving in day-to-day experiences. The best way to do this is by modeling it as parents (Heb. 11:6).

SEVENTEEN: Should I expect bigger blessings if I give?

If you ask such a question, probably not. Anyone who gives to get is a selfish giver. Plus, this kind of false doctrine falls under the demonic belief of prosperity doctrine. God rewards those whom He chooses. My experience is that He is not quick to reward any child of His with a "give to get" motive. We should not give with any expectation of man or God, even though God is known for blessing His givers. Our motives need to be pure in advancing the kingdom of God.

Where is your money going? Is it being dumped into making the rich richer through paying interest on your debt? Is it advancing the kingdom of Satan by drinking, drugging, and sexing it away? Is it being donated to charitable causes that mean absolutely nothing to God? You are the one who has to examine your giving record, or lack of it. God loves a cheerful giver, but He will never bless a donor dollar that benefits the kindness of the Antichrist. Did that sound a bit odd? It should. The Antichrist will be so kind and prone to giving that the whole world will be donating every spare dollar it can to bless his efforts, which will burn up in the final fire of purification. He will require others to give to him, but he will by no means give unto others. He is a taker of takers. Which side are you on? Something to think about…

CHAPTER 18

WHY STAY OUT OF DEBT

Did you know the original meaning for "mortgage" is "dead pledge?" To "amortize" means "to deaden." Did you know that one of the 13 names for Satan is "debt?" It is true. This is why Jesus needed to come and "pay our debt that we could not pay" (Col. 2:13-14).

The Hebrew word picture for debt is "mem-tav": "mem" is a picture of flooding waters and "tav" is a sign of the cross, meaning "what God had promised would happen because of sin." Satan (debt) is a master of bondage, which creates death. The enemy's goal has always been to create so much debt that it is impossible for the individual to pay it back. Debt (Satan) creates a relationship of servitude and slavery to the one who offered the apple of death. Satan does not care what kind of debt one adopts: money, promises, material things, food, time, tithe, favors, or sins. It really doesn't matter to him!

In the Old Testament times, loaning money to fellow Jewish brothers was only under the condition of charitable giving. It was absolutely forbidden (still is) to charge interest to a brother of the race. The children of God were not to borrow, or loan, to people outside their race. If they did, they were accused of forming partnerships with the "unequally yoked." The early Jews knew the interest charged would create long-term bondage. Under Hebraic law, if a person loaned money to a brother and he refused (or couldn't) pay it back, the loan was then considered "charitable giving." This was not determined until the end of the seventh year. If the borrower was caught a second time "stiffing" a fellow brother for a loan, he was to be treated as a foreigner. This included no financial dealings, which would force him to leave the community.

Nowadays, when an individual cannot pay a debt, he considers ideas such as bankruptcy. Bankruptcy is not a biblical solution, nor does God support these kinds of resolutions. Bankruptcy laws are changing to make it easier for individuals and corporations to go this route. It used to be when a person went bankrupt, his assets were turned into legal tender and the money would be used to pay down the debt. The Hebrew Word Picture for bankrupt is "broken bench." It was a custom to do business while sitting on a bench, which was usually located in the courtyard of the temple. Back then, when a banker went "bankrupt" his bench was broken by other businessmen. This is actually the practice that Jesus was addressing when he threw the "money changers" out of the temple (Matt. 21:12). As the years have passed, bankruptcy has become a way of escaping from the responsibility of paying debt. God tells us to "be in debt to no man" and to pay up all of our debts, unless we are forgiven of that debt.

Depreciating Debt Items: The worst kind of debt is money owed on items that decrease in value the longer one looks at them. The longer one owns them, the more worthless they become. Since with most debt there is interest, with these depreciating debts, a person is actually throwing his money to the wind. Jesus graciously reminds us of these worthless investments:

" *'Do not store up for yourselves treasures on earth, where moth and rust destroy, and where thieves break in and steal'* " (Matt. 6:19).

He is speaking of depreciating items that collect dust and moths. So what are these appreciating items? Let's take a look.

Appreciating Items: It used to be when someone bought a house or land, he was guaranteed to be investing in an appreciating item. The closer we get to the end-times and the final global economy, we are going to find that even gold and silver are going to be bad investments. God made it clear to us that wisdom and understanding is so much better than gold and silver (Prov.16:16). He also promises that those who seek wisdom and understanding are considered wealthy in the kingdom of God. For most "Christians," this isn't enough. They want more – much more. They want the best of both worlds. Up until most recently, that plan has worked fairly well. Soon and very soon, "Christians" will be faced with having to choose which master they will serve. But for now, they can claim the prosperity of two masters and get away with it.

"Your gold and your silver have rusted; and their rust will be a witness against you and will consume your flesh like fire. It is in the last days that you have stored up your treasure" (James 5:3)!

James is openly warning us about storing up gold and silver for the end-times. I know many "Christians" who are buying up gold and silver. They are hoping that "if" the economy falls out, they will have some assets with "appreciating value" that will care for them in tough times. The problem with that solution is there are multiple passages in the Bible in which God says He is going to make gold and silver worthless. Secondly, Revelation tells us that true indwelt Christians will not be able to "buy, sell, or trade" in this final system of the Antichrist. So what is a true Christian to do? That is where we are going in this book – keep reading!

Did you know that when we are using that credit card, or borrowing money from the lender, we are not only spending someone else's money, but we are dragging around a "carrus" full of bags? The Roman pagans used a system of charging in order to enslave others to be their baggage carriers. If one borrowed from a Roman, he would be required to be his "baggage wagon" carrier until his debt was paid in full. This is where we get the Latin definition of "carrus/charge," which means "baggage wagon." It is through this early Roman practice that I get the Revelation Roman Empire practice of the Antichrist enslaving the world to his baggage cart. I believe that personal, corporate, and national debt is the number one requirement for slavery to the Antichrist. For without debt, the people are freed from being a baggage toting "donkey" for the Antichrist, and I mean that literally.

Compounding Interest: Satan is not satisfied with you and me being in debt with a bit of interest piled on top. He is really after the compounding interest. When we get caught by this trap, we begin to feel like we will never be out of debt and oftentimes never are. Cumulus, or compound, debt is exactly what the word means: to pile up one upon another. If we get behind in a payment, the compounding interest kicks in and we soon find ourselves only being able to make the interest payments and never (or rarely) touching the principle debt. This is the condition that most credit card toting slaves are in today. I, too, was once a credit card slave; more than once, in fact. Once Satan has us paying the interest payment only, he then can come in with his left-handed punch through the loss of a job, health problems, car repairs, or any other kind of "emergency" that justifies more debt. His goal – financial disaster and spiritual, emotional, and financial bondage!

Do you remember me mentioning earlier the true to life facts about how much interest the United States of America pays per second on our national debt (not including our internal debt)? To refresh our minds, I will reiterate those numbers. The U.S. is charged compounding interest to the tune of $41 million per hour. To make it even more real: that's $984 million per day, $690,000 per minute, or $11,500 per second! This is why even our unsaved global economists are saying that America will never be able to get out of debt. No big deal, right? Hmm, I'm not even going to comment on that one!

God graciously warned us and then He told us. Now we are beginning to suffer the ultimate consequences of borrowing. God gave His guidelines of:

"Owe nothing to anyone except to love one another; for he who loves his neighbor has fulfilled the law" (Rom. 13:8).

This is not only something that is required of the private sector, but every nation on the face of the earth is soon to tote this wagon. Today, when people have to choose between loving someone and getting that new "thing," statistics prove they choose debt.

I have reviewed some of the proposals of the G-20 debt reduction plan. One of the more sobering items is that all the debt accumulated by parents will require payment by their children and grandchildren – up to four generations! Once the Antichrist's system is implemented, every time we use that credit card we are potentially putting our great-great-grandchildren in debt. Shocking? Well, that is how national debt works. We pass it from President to President and generation to generation. Why hasn't the world up to this point made a big deal about our trillions of dollars of debt? Some have. But the reason there has not been a global outcry is because the Antichrist has wanted to turn the interest into compound interest. Now that the debt is so out of control, a leader can step in and suggest an idea that will "miraculously" set us free from certain global disaster.

The Curse Coming Down Upon Us: So far, we have mostly been dealing with the negative issues relating to the Antichrist and debt. But we must not forget about the judgment of God. God is clear about how He handles people or nations that are in debt.

"But it shall come about, if you do not obey the LORD your God, to observe to do all His commandments and His statutes with which I charge you today, that all these curses will come upon you and overtake you: 'He shall lend to you, but you will not lend to him; he shall be the head, and you will be the tail' " (Deut. 28:15, 44).

Who exactly is He talking about here? The "you" is anyone who is disobedient to the Lord's commands. If you and I think these "curses" are locked in the Old Testament, then we do not understand the purpose of the Old Testament. The curse still applies to all unsaved people or nations who have not been freed through the power of the Cross – Salvation. God is already allowing these "curses" to come upon the people of the world and they ARE continuously overtaking them. If you don't believe me, check out the world news tonight. God goes on to warn us that this "he" will lend to us, but we will not be able to lend to him. Why? This "he" (Antichrist) is going to be the "head" of the dog and the unsaved people are going to be the "tail." When the head decides to wag, all the people will wag.

What should not be news to you and me by now is that the borrower is a slave to the lender (Prov. 22:7). One of the primal ways for God to keep His children from being slaves after Salvation is by keeping them out of debt! God would like for all of His precious children to be 100% free from the affairs of everyday life. God knows, because He made us, that our calling requires service and loyalty to the one who enlisted us into our calling. He certainly would like for us to understand that DEBT distracts us from that reality. Debt deceptively forces us to shift our loyalty (and kingdom monies) to a "new commander and chief."

"No soldier in active service entangles himself in the affairs of everyday life, so that he may please the one who enlisted him as a soldier" (2 Tim. 2:4).

CHAPTER 19

DEBT CONTROLS OUR PAST, PRESENT & FUTURE

Many of our financial moves are based upon our lack of trust in God, the Father, having Sovereign control over our past, present, and future. In fact, debt is rooted in the fear that if we don't control our present, then our future will become gainfully out of control. Fear of the future causes people to make rash decisions, which oftentimes require years of slavery. Whether we are spenders, hoarders, or both – fear is certainly one of the most expensive choices in the entire universe.

"Come now, you who say, 'Today or tomorrow we will go to such and such a city, and spend a year there and engage in business and make a profit.' Yet you do not know what your life will be like tomorrow. You are just a vapor that appears for a little while and then vanishes away. Instead, you ought to say, 'If the Lord wills, we will live and also do this or that' " (James 4:13-15).

My experience is that most men live and breathe this deception. They get up each day ready to wage war with the marketplace, trying to make a profit. How many people do we know who are NOT caught up in this lie? Most men look at life in general through the eyeglasses of profit. Occasionally I will meet someone who really and honestly believes that "if God wills it – I will do it." Part of this dynamic is because men are called by God to be providers. But when we step over into illusive self-confidence, we activate God's obligatory actions of showing us that we are only vapors, which are soon to vanish. The sooner we embrace the truth that we have no control over the past, present, and future; the closer we will be to peace.

I AM MY OWN BOSS: The problem with the goal mentality of engaging in business to make a profit is that it gives the temporary illusion of independence from God's authority. Once a person starts living this illusive lie, his decisions begin to "shortchange" God's passionate desire to be his provider. God will allow the illusion to wear the person down, until his dream becomes a nightmare. God doesn't want His children to feel that they are in control of their own lives – or dare to think they can form their own version of authority! ALL authority that does exist, exists because of God – for He is authority. The word authority means the "author who acts." If we take this meaning to be literal, and we should, anyone who makes up his own version of authority is committing the same sin Satan did right before he was tossed out of heaven. He thought he was God.

Retaining the position of not needing the wisdom that God gives His authority figures (patriarchs, fathers, pastors, and counselors), nor the wisdom of God Himself (directly through His written Word) is the result of a person living like this. A mind-set like this literally condemns God and confesses that he is an arrogant person who is practicing sin.

"But as it is, you boast in your arrogance; all such boasting is evil. Therefore, to one who knows the right thing to do and does not do it, to him it is sin" (James 4:16-17).

Most define sin as an action that purposes to side against God, like stealing. Few define it as not doing something. Once God shows us the right thing to do and we simply don't do it, we are practicing SIN. There are many walking around in sin, 24/7. When a man confuses this principle, God typically begins withholding funds and for good reason. I must say though, most take this as a challenge and try all the harder to "beat the system." God's response: He fixes a bigger fix to stop the person from fixing the fix that God has fixed on him. No need to panic; this is a sign that God is in the process of evaluating our lives, our plans for His money, and ultimately, our faith in Him.

People who mishandle God's money, and I'm not talking about the tithe, cause undue pressure upon those who are supposedly dependent on them for leadership, provision, and protection. These individuals are quick to use "their authority" to rule others, but are quicker to rebel when it comes to authority figures in their lives. This is why followers do not trust them and find it almost impossible to follow and obey them. Your average follower knows that the hardship and consequences the leader incurs can transfer to the dependents. The emotive burden of this factor is so overwhelming, in most cases, it leads to a divorce – either personally or businesswise. Debt is a generational fixture; it is passed like a torch from one generation to the next. It is only selfish leaders who do not put an end to this oppressive factor.

BLOCKING GOD'S PROTECTION AND PROVISION: The simple fact is: all God really wants is for each of us to submit to Him as Abba Father. It really is a simple plan – He is the Father and we are His children. When we begin to function as spiritual sons and daughters, He begins supernaturally showing His power through the lives of His children (us). If the child is more comfortable serving under the "father of lies," well, that is exactly who He allows. Everyone needs a daddy and everyone submits to one. The question then becomes, "Who's your daddy?"

The big difference between the two "daddies" is that Satan wants "his kids" to think they are the boss, while he leads them around by the ring in their noses. God, on the other hand, will never sit back and allow His child to think, fall, or function in independence. God, as a Father, will never share His glory with anyone. Satan shares his glory all day long with those who do not have a pure heart. But in the end, he will call in all those who are in debt to him. In those days he (Satan) will require full loyalty, submission, and obedience; even from the most rebellious types in the world. Every tough guy has a breaking point – even Satan. That is why I have such compassion for the bullies of the world. God and Satan know that they (bullies) are scared little nobodies who demand to be somebody.

DROWNING IN DESTRUCTION: When we are enslaved to the enemy through debt, it blocks us from experiencing the full blessings of the living God. The primary reason we buy things on, or off, credit is because we believe these things will benefit our lives, even though deep down inside we know they are unnecessary. As any good father, He limits our funding so we cannot purchase such temporary fixes. When we move through His barriers and purchase them anyway, ON CREDIT, we are confessing to James 4:3:

"You ask and do not receive, because you ask with wrong motives, so that you may spend it on your pleasures" (James 4:3).

Wouldn't God be as a fool if He gave funding to us to purchase "things" for selfish pleasure? Since God will never be as a fool, we can be assured He will do what He is able to stop us from purchasing selfishly. If we decide to push through the blockage, then a new dimension to God's guidance opens up to us.

"But those who want to get rich fall into temptation and a snare and many foolish and harmful desires which plunge men into ruin and destruction" (1 Tim. 6:9).

Here is the key: God faithfully puts the roadblocks in place while we are yet on the road. But when we push through the barrier and fall into the hole of temptation, He steps back and allows the consequences (ruin and destruction) of our fall to be the temporary father to parent us. This kind of discipline seems to be harsh and unreasonable, at first. But those who learn to endure by it will ultimately grow in righteousness.

CHAPTER 20

CARMEL COVERED ROTTING APPLES

One of my favorite treats is a caramel covered apple, particularly those with crushed goodies on top. Recently as I was contemplating our topic, God gave me an example that clearly communicates how the enemy deceives us into debt thinking. When Eve was looking upon the Tree of Knowledge of Good and Evil and gazing at that dangling apple, I think she was seeing a pile of sin covered with the caramel of lust. The real apple, the one from the Tree of Life, is God's provision of food and clothing, coated and dipped in contentment.

"If we have food and covering, with these we shall be content" (1 Tim. 6:8).

The apple from Satan's tree comes in all sizes and forms, but his method of operation is always predictable. Any kind of want beyond these two basic elements of life, begins the temptation process of the "caramel apple." A fact that has always amazed me is that Satan actually makes people go into debt to eat from his tree – and people are willing to borrow to do it. The food from God's tree is free and is spiritually and organically good for us.

It is not uncommon to find people who actually use credit to pay for the basic necessities of life. Only 25 years ago, that would have been quite uncommon. But today, 90% of credit card holders won't even think twice about it. If people are using credit to purchase food and clothing, we can be fairly certain the money God IS providing to cover the two basics of life is being mismanaged.

Does something strike you a bit wrong about that picture? It would be like your father giving you five dollars to go to the grocer to buy milk and bread and you come back with candy. Then he sends you back to the store to exchange the candy for the milk and bread, you eat the candy on the way, and buy the milk and bread on your "dad's account." What child would do that? A child who believes his father will "grace" them on all stupid decisions.

"For the love of money is a root of all sorts of evil, and some by longing for it have wandered away from the faith and pierced themselves with many griefs" (1 Tim. 6:10).

This scenario reveals the state of our church today. Most "children of God" treat God like He is some kind of slot machine. This generation of believers uses grace like it is some "get out of jail free card," somehow thinking that God is turning a blind eye to the child. It is this kind of child who will grow into an adult, who will borrow money to buy food and clothing – and cars, boats, tools, vacations, repairs, and anything else that is pleasing to the eye. It is easy to understand that a child does not have the comprehension of the final price tag of using someone else's money to live. But as adults, we should expect children to embrace the error of living in terms of monthly payments.

MONTHLY PAYMENT CHRISTIANS: People who borrow to live usually get in the nasty habit of looking at the interest as such a small amount of money – while thinking that every loan is a short-term loan. This is "stinking thinking" for sure. In reality, the interest payments constitute a very large part of the total cost of the loan. Most of the time, people pay three times more for an item than it is worth, when they borrow to get it. God is not in support of His people throwing His money into the winds of interest.

What God does expect is for His children to be good stewards of His money. The way we find a faithful steward is through the measurement God gives us in the Scriptures; he who is faithful with the small things can be entrusted to much.

" 'And I say to you, make friends for yourselves by means of the wealth of unrighteousness, so that when it fails, they will receive you into the eternal dwellings. He who is faithful in a very little thing is faithful also in much; and he who is unrighteous in a very little thing is unrighteous also in much' " (Luke 16:9-10).

Those who live by the "monthly payment" trap should fear for their future. It is a self-rewarding system. Each time one pays off a loan, he is tricked into thinking he can pay off the next one and then the next. The problem with this kind of thinking is it does not count the cost of expenditures outside the budget, particularly emergency ones. This is why we need to set aside emergency monies each month – even if it is only $5 per month. Emergency expenditures are Satan's second phase of his plan to throw a person into more debt. A simple plan, but it works almost 100% of the time.

When a person is in debt, he cannot use normal and natural resources to get those little extras. For example: When a person is in debt, any levelheaded counselor is going to advise him to sell off everything he can to pay down that debt – and he should. If a man who has no debt wants that particular "toy" or tool, he could sell something he no longer uses, or wants, to purchase the item he desires. This kind of budgeting is common sense living in God's miraculous plan of economy. A man or woman who lives like this is free mentally, emotionally, and spiritually before the Lord and man. But I'm afraid this will never happen as long as the person is trapped in impulse buying.

I have come to learn, the hard way, that God wants us to pray about all of our decisions, particularly the financial ones. The reason for this is He is the One who actually gave us the money to be stewarded in the first place. We need to be perfectly clear how He would like us to invest His resources. Debt, on the other hand, would not survive without impulse buying – buying without praying and actually getting an answer. Satan is making it easier and easier to get borrowed money, so we can call it ours. If the world made it difficult to get someone else's cash, the enemy would lose his footing in impulsivity. He certainly is not about to let that happen. Therefore, he will continue to make it easy to access other people's money in order for borrowers to live. The end result is that people will not seek out wise counsel and prayerful considerations; thus, never getting to know the mind of God.

"Also it is not good for a person to be without knowledge, and he who hurries his footsteps errs" (Prov. 19:2).

People who are rushed with decisions usually end up hanging with like-minded people who keep their slide oiled for destruction.

DON'T PANIC, GOD WILL PROVIDE: They tell me that the majority of people don't believe this literally; but for the sake of their reputations, they say they do. God has promised to provide for His children no matter what the child believes.

"And my God will supply all your needs according to His riches in glory in Christ Jesus" (Phil. 4:19).

Debt mentality is a covert form of saying, "God really won't take care of all my needs!" In reality, the person is actually saying, "God will not give me all *I want*." Needs are relative, unless we look at them through the eyes of God. When God's children rely on credit cards, they are slapping the Hand that is to feed them. Most don't wait long enough to discover if this "feeling" is a want or a need. It usually takes God to determine if a desire is a need. Even if we have the cash to purchase the item, it does not mean that God will approve the purchase. The only way to truly know if a purchase is God's will is to unreservedly trust Him to provide the funds ahead of time. That type of living requires faith, the kind that pleases God.

"And without faith it is impossible to please Him, for he who comes to God must believe that He is and that He is a rewarder of those who seek Him" (Heb.11:6).

BALANCING OUT ABUNDANCE AND NEED: One of the common ways we see God providing for someone who is in need, and at times in want, is by the increase of a particular Christian. He moves upon the heart of the abundant one to give to the hands of the needy. Too simple? Not for me! In fact, it is God's miraculous plan for His economy. He causes one to increase in order to give to the one who is in decrease. When the decreased one starts on the increase, He uses that increased one to bless another, who is in decrease. Sooner or later the cycle begins to feed itself. What typically happens is the selfish flesh usually stops the food chain, the system breaks down, and people revert to debt. God is all about interdependence.

"At this present time your abundance being a supply for their need, so that their abundance also may become a supply for your need, that there may be equality; as

it is written, 'HE WHO gathered MUCH DID NOT HAVE TOO MUCH, AND HE WHO gathered LITTLE HAD NO LACK' " (2 Cor. 8:14-15).

Credit card mentality people become over-spenders of God's eternal resources and ultimately, cannot be trusted by God or others. Not only do they overspend, but they pay too much for the items they impulsively buy. Debt people are never satisfied with what they have; they always want more. God has told us many times that those who love silver shall not be satisfied with that silver, nor will people who love the abundance of things (Eccl. 5:10). Solomon learned that lesson the hard way.

CHAPTER 21

LEARNING TO BE WELL CONTENT

Most "Christians" today have the covert belief that external hardship is a sign of discipline or lack of approval from God. While this can be true, the Emergent Postmodern world today touts that true success is evidenced by prosperity and popularity. Did you know that if the biblical Paul lived today, he would most likely be despised by today's Christian church? It's true! Paul was preaching a gospel that invited pain and suffering. In fact, he was preaching a message stating that we should question our faith if we're not suffering external hardships.

Paul went from being one, if not the most, prosperous and popular religious person in the world, to being one of the most despised. Every time Paul turned around, he was faced with either being persecuted or having something fall down around him.

"Are they servants of Christ?--I speak as if insane--I more so; in far more labors, in far more imprisonments, beaten times without number, often in danger of death. Five times I received from the Jews thirty-nine lashes. Three times I was beaten with rods, once I was stoned, three times I was shipwrecked, a night and a day I have spent in the deep. I have been on frequent journeys, in dangers from rivers, dangers from robbers, dangers from my countrymen, dangers from the Gentiles, dangers in the city, dangers in the wilderness, dangers on the sea, dangers among false brethren; I have been in labor and hardship, through many sleepless nights, in hunger and thirst, often without food, in cold and exposure" (2 Cor. 11:23-27).

Let's face it, if you and I were to look upon a Christian leader today with this list: endless labors, imprisonments, beatings with rods, brushes with death, whippings, stonings, shipwrecks, floating in the sea for a day, dangers of rivers, robberies, dangers from his own people and townspeople, attacks in the wilderness, betrayal of false brethren, hardships, sleepless nights, hunger, thirst, and cold – we probably would tell him God was punishing him. Where do we get such "stinky thinking?" We get it from the enemy, of course. God wants us to learn to be well content with all things – good and not so good. We usually associate this with financial success, but God is actually referencing *all* forms of suffering and circumstances.

"Not that I speak from want, for I have learned to be content in whatever circumstances I am. I know how to get along with humble means, and I also know how to live in prosperity; in any and every circumstance I have learned the secret of being filled and going hungry, both of having abundance and suffering need" (Phil. 4:11-12).

Up until recently, postmodern Christians have been able to escape this message of Truth. But soon, all people will be faced with the consequences of global debt. Before long, the prosperity Christians who believe popularity equals success will be faced with a global crisis. This will force humility and cause them to turn an ear to teachers who preach the same message of our beloved Paul. There is such arrogance in our brethren today; it is easy to see a great humbling is coming.

Most believers (indwelt Christians) don't really know the difference between poverty and wealth. This is why God is committed to showing His people the difference. Some of the most arrogant accusers I have had to face in my ministry life have been "believers" who refuse to associate with me because of my beliefs regarding poverty and prosperity. Even though this is a sad commentary for me, I understand that our society has touted capitalism to the point of its invasion into the Church.

Since God is a jealous God (Ex. 20:5), when a man falls into the lie that he can provide for himself or his family on his own, He knows it is time for a lesson. It is difficult living out the biblical mandates of prosperity and poverty under a banner of capitalism. Capitalism shouts out through an economic system that says "production through private ownership equals profit." The lie pervading the American society is "if you're not a capitalist, you are a socialist." This is the furthest thing from the truth – at least for true indwelt Christians. Satan has installed a fear into postmodern Christians that if they live out the model of body-life prosperity in the Bible, they somehow will be supporting Socialism. I mean seriously, look at this:

"For there was not a needy person among them, for all who were owners of land or houses would sell them and bring the proceeds of the sales and lay them at the apostles' feet, and they would be distributed to each as any had need" (Acts 4:34-35).

That almost sounds like a "Jimmy Jones" cult practice. I consider these two verses to be some of the most radical in the entire Bible. What would you do if you found your neighbor selling his house to give the money to a needy person in his church? Wouldn't you be tempted to accuse him of being in a cult? I have surveyed this and 95% of the Christians questioned said "yes" to the "cult" status.

Either Jesus Himself is an exaggerator or He is speaking the Truth when He says: " 'Sell your possessions and give to charity; make yourselves money belts which do not wear out, an unfailing treasure in heaven, where no thief comes near nor moth destroys' " (Luke 12:33; also see Matt. 19:21, Mark 10:21, Luke 18:22 & 25, Rev. 13:17).

Until we get closer to the end-times, I really don't think the average Christian is going to get what Jesus and the rest of the New Testament characters are saying regarding caring for the body of Christ, without a heavy reliance upon a worldly system of temporal gain. The movement we are going to be seeing over the next 20 + years is this: The "Truth-saying" prophet-type teachers of the Word are going to be called upon more than ever before. What many of our stabile prophecy interpreters have been saying is now actually coming true. This will even be more of the case as the enemy unfolds his evil, yet tastefully delicious, plan to the world. The danger to this new movement is that the "false prophets" will be coming out of the woodwork like never before. This is why we MUST encourage the indwelt Christians to get back into the Word and stabilize their beliefs according to the written Word of God.

Have you ever noticed how large income people never have enough money to pay their bills? The reason is they tend to spend their money on people, places, and things that have nothing to do with how God allows them to spend their money. Since a man's heart is where his money is invested, we are quickly able to see the heart of a man by telling him what he CAN'T spend his money on. Usually, he will manifest an attitude that proves his irresponsibility – "You can't tell me how to spend my money!" These types of money spenders are poor in the eyes of God, no matter how much is in their bank accounts.

People, who are aroused in rebellion when told NOT to spend their money in a certain way, typically think that making more money will make him/her wealthier. Proverbs calls this kind of man a fool. There is much more to making and keeping money than just putting one's mind to becoming rich, or even becoming "sufficiently satisfied."

"Who is there who speaks and it comes to pass, unless the Lord has commanded it?" (Lam. 3:37).

A fool can "name it and claim it" all day long, day after day, and nothing will become of it unless the Lord decides so. Even in this decision of the Lord, He will decide for a fool to become prosperous for two distinctly different reasons: one, to cause success in order to bring him to nothingness (take it all away) and secondly, to ultimately give it to the children of God. I can assure you that while the fool is on his prosperity path, he thinks nothing can stop him and nobody can tell him how to spend "his money." As soon as a man thinks his income is his own, he has lost touch with God's reality. When that happens, the man is about to face a strong wind.

" 'You look for much, but behold, it comes to little; when you bring it home, I blow it away. Why?' declares the LORD of hosts, 'Because of My house which lies desolate, while each of you runs to his own house' " (Hag. 1:9).

What we see here is the design and purpose of poverty and prosperity – according to God. If the man looks for an increase in wealth, God will work to bring it to little and sometimes will toss the hard earned money right to the wind (nothingness). Why? As the verse mentions, God is all about building His own house. Most people, who focus on making money, usually forget this and spend their "hard earned money" on either securing a nest egg or getting out of debt in order to go into debt once again. It is called "using credit to secure credit." What the debt facilitators are really saying is "go into debt, to go into more debt." This is why it is a vicious cycle of bondage. Those who have been there more than once know exactly what I'm saying.

Hopefully, we are now able to see that the loss of money can be God's divine intervention and discipline for those who refuse to spend His money on what God allows. God is a "cause and effect" God when it comes to violating His laws and losing cash flow (see Prov. 5:10; 6:11; 10:3-4; 11:5, 24, 29; 13:11,18; 14:23; 19:15; 21:13, 17; 22:16; 23:21; 28:8; 19, 22).

I know personally it is a difficult reality to embrace that God causes some to be rich and some to be poor. God has His reasons for choosing different means and people to accomplish different purposes for His glory.

CHAPTER 22

THE RICH VERSUS THE POOR

It is so easy to get caught up in questions like: "Does God want certain people rich and others poor?" The truth is, God isn't into some being rich and others being poor. His divine will is for the world to focus upon His eternal riches. It is true that in this process He will temporarily allow wealth with some, in order to help with the poverty of others. Scriptures show us that He doesn't do this to increase the wealth of one, but rather to keep his promise of feeding and clothing ALL of His creation. If every human used his extra cash (anything above living expenses) to feed and clothe another human, I can assure you – there would NOT be one single hungry or naked person in the entire world! In order for this principle to really produce fruit, it would require a spreading of the world's wealth with such equality that there would no longer be sharp differences in corporate or privatized income.

Since we will never see the above principle lived out on this earth, greed will continue to rule the world. God will continue allowing people and nations to increase in their wealth, so He can humble them by causing them to lose their riches. Usually it only takes a disaster or two to bring a thriving economy (personally or nationally) to its knees. Even in my small life span, I have seen some of the richest people and nations in the world go broke overnight. For those who follow Him through the indwelling power of His Son, He oftentimes causes loss of money, so that they might discover the full on riches and provisions of God's miraculous plan of economy.

"You made men ride over our heads; we went through fire and through water, yet You brought us out into a place of abundance" (Psalm 66:12).

GOVERNMENT BAILOUTS: I really don't mean to sound rude or coldhearted, but people really are like stupid sheep! God works so diligently to create dependence on Him. But what do they do? They run to government programs, like sheep being lead to a slaughterhouse. Poverty will never be eliminated or helped through special social programs. If I remember correctly, the definition of insanity is doing the same thing over and over again – thinking the next time you do it, things will be different. I don't know if you have noticed or not, but the trillions and trillions of dollars we throw at poverty are NOT fixing the problem. In fact, let's take America as an example. Statistics prove that even though we spend more and more on social welfare each year, poverty is actually getting worse. Social programs, which are purposed to end poverty, usually make big government and the idea makers richer. Plus, it negates what God wants to accomplish through the individual and national poverty rate (like honest appraisal, seeking the Lord God, and Body-Life dependence). Do you want a simpleminded definition of politics? Men like power and power is not realized for an individual or nation unless there is someone(s) begging at their feet.

Did you know that a cow eats enough food to feed seven people? There are an estimated 350 million "sacred cows" in India? If we do the math, we will find that if the people would stop feeding the cows their food, they would have enough food to feed well over a billion people. If they turned the cows into hamburger, they would generate an export that could stabilize the entire country. Satan might be stupid, but he knows what he is doing! He would rather the people worship a cow and go hungry, than meet the needs of his followers. Idolatry always ultimately starves its followers. Once hungry, they come begging at the king's (Antichrist's) table.

If we replace the cow with other types of idols, we will find the same kind of stupidity in every country in the world. Idols truly make people lethargic and almost stupid to common sense.

LAZY PEOPLE USUALLY GO HUNGRY: This is a truth that is argued over throughout the halls of history. This simple fact is: if you don't work – you don't eat!

"For even when we were with you, we used to give you this order: if anyone is not willing to work, then he is not to eat, either" (2 Thess. 3:10).

Sounds kind of rude and cruel doesn't it? In God's plan of economy, these two principles go hand in hand. It is primarily because of this reason that I continued to work in some fashion or another throughout my heart failure experience, even while I was in the hospital. A lazy person is not necessarily someone who rejects the idea of labor, but rather someone who procrastinates in doing it.

"A little sleep, a little slumber, a little folding of the hands to rest -- your poverty will come in like a vagabond and your need like an armed man" (Prov. 6:10-11).

In over 30 years of counseling the hurting, procrastinators (lazy people) are the worst kind of people to deal with. They nod their heads "yes" on the outside, but delay on the inside. When confronted about their laziness, they typically justify their behavior by an endless list of reasons why they could not do what was asked of them. Meanwhile, they put the responsibility on the "counselor" to fix the fix they actually fixed on themselves and then get frustrated, or downright angry, if the "counselor" doesn't. Working with the lazy is like trying to make a pathway through a bowl of jello.

"The sluggard (lazy) does not plow after the autumn, so he begs during the harvest and has nothing" (Prov. 20:4, parentheses mine).

We see in the Scriptures that God purposes to bring "nothingness" to lazy people throughout the world - because they won't, or refuse, to work for food. I cannot tell you how many times I have been asked the question as to why God allows poverty and hungry people in the world. We have poverty in the world because people would rather give the five bucks than hire the man to work for his food. It is not any more complicated than that. We are literally causing the lazy to become dependent on BIG government. If you haven't noticed, government sponsored social welfare DOES NOT WORK!

Don't get me wrong, God does command us to take care of the poor, but He does NOT want us to give without prayer and supplication. Much of the poor are poor because of circumstances outside of their control: health issues, widows, orphans, employment issues, etc. We are required by God to assist and care for the truly needy. If we were able to separate the workers from the truly needy and put the workers to work, we wouldn't have the massive problem of poverty that we have today. In fact, God usually sides with the truly poor and if any come against them, He takes those actions personally.

"He who oppresses the poor taunts his Maker, but he who is gracious to the needy honors Him" (Prov. 14:31).

If you want to taunt God, God forbid, just ignore the poor in your community!! If you dare to "make a buck" off of the poor, God is certain to put you in want!

"He who oppresses the poor to make more for himself or who gives to the rich, will only come to poverty" (Prov. 22:16).

Allow me to give you an example of this truth. Recently, the second wealthiest country in the world had a tsunami-causing major earthquake. These two catastrophic events washed out a major portion of the country, leading to potential life-threatening impairments in several nuclear reactors (releasing hazardous chemicals, damaging much of the food supply, and resulting in very long food lines). Another country, who is in financial debt to this traumatized country, offered $200 million of food and medical supplies at the price of more debt to its own people. Is this really the right thing to do? Was this country giving to the rich, who could afford their own bailout? What are the consequences of such actions as feeding the rich? I can tell you – the country giving $200 million dollars will only come to poverty! If we are honest with ourselves, we know why country CHAPTER 2 was feeding the rich. But should a country ever take care of the poverty needs of another country while ignoring the poverty needs of their own people? Of course not! But most countries will "kowtow" like this every time there is any kind of global crisis. Anytime an individual or nation gives to others while oppressing their own people, God WILL bring judgment upon them.

"You shall not afflict any widow or orphan. If you afflict him at all, and if he does cry out to Me, I will surely hear his cry; and My anger will be kindled, and I will kill you with the sword, and your wives shall become widows and your children fatherless" (Ex. 22:22-24).

Hmm – so why exactly is our world being filled with widows, fatherless children, poverty, and despair?

CHAPTER 23

RESPONSIBILITIES OF THE FAMILY

GOVERNMENT SUPPLIED JOBS: Just as it is in each of the divisions of the Department of Social Welfare, it is NOT the responsibility of the government to find jobs for the needy. The biblical reason and purpose of government is for God to have a system of justice to oversee His laws and to deliver the consequences when His commands are not honored. I'm not sure you will find any country in the world that has set the purpose of their government to do that. One of my favorite passages that can help us understand the purpose of government is in 2 Peter. Check this out:

"Submit yourselves for the Lord's sake to every human institution, whether to a king as the one in authority, or to governors as sent by Him for the punishment of evildoers and the praise of those who do right" (1 Peter 2:13-14).

God clearly reveals in this passage the purpose for earthly government. When government steps out of its bounds and attempts to manage the hearts and morality of the people, BIG government is formed.

Once a government is functioning in its God-given boundaries, the local business owners are free to hire and fire according to their individual goals and beliefs. As soon as the government tries to manage the corporate sector, business owners begin to feel like their hands are being tied through government regulations. Once that happens, business owners can't fire, hire, or manage workers according to their beliefs; but rather, the workers start managing the employers according to workers' "rights." Then, government is upside down and the people who are actually responsible for keeping unemployment out of the dumper are being led around as if they have rings in their noses. The ultimate consequence for the employer is that they won't "feel led" to leave a portion of their profits to the poor.

" *'Now when you reap the harvest of your land, you shall not reap to the very corners of your field, nor shall you gather the gleanings of your harvest. Nor shall you glean your vineyard, nor shall you gather the fallen fruit of your vineyard; you shall leave them for the needy and for the stranger. I am the LORD your God' "* (Lev. 19:9-10).

If you read the above two verses, you just saw one of the all-time solutions to poverty. Since we have BIG government managing small businesses through policies, poverty will only increase. The reason employers don't leave a portion of their businesses for the poor to feed off of is because they feel like they are being taxed to death before they even hire their first employee. When you open your morning paper tomorrow, read all the headlines! Review just how much of the news is over this topic. You should discover the majority of news is over the privatization rights of small business.

GOVERNMENT PAYOUTS: Another topic you will read about frequently in the news is in regard to "government payouts." Is it biblical to guarantee monthly income like Social Security checks? NO – it is not scriptural. Not only does this support the idea of BIG government, but it destroys personal responsibility and multigenerational family integration. Even though it is NOT free money, it feels like free money to the slothful (lazy). While it promotes laziness in some, it also causes erosion and destruction of the original structure of family. God puts the full responsibility of caring for the elderly and needy on family. If the family is unable to care for their elders and needy family members, they are to go to the church. The church elders are then to assign another family(ies) to help train and care for those who have needy members under their roofs. That leads us to the topic of nursing homes.

NURSING HOMES: Does the Bible support the idea of nursing homes? I am afraid not! I know that our postmodern structure makes it almost "impossible" to care for our elderly parents; but it doesn't change the truth.

Multigenerational care is not a new concept – not at all. From the design of the original Hebrew family to that of Jesus going and preparing a place for His bride "in His Father's house," it has been the norm of God to conduct family business in this fashion.

So – what happened to us? Satan has so fractured God's original design of family, elder care, and social welfare of the needy, that we have become depraved to the point of shipping our parents off to institutions and paying for others to finish what was originally our responsibility. In many of these cases, the families don't even pay for these services; but rather, put the government in the position of having to come up with the money to do what God is asking the children to do. It is no wonder why the government is trying to pass legislation to euthanize (medically kill) our elderly. Just from an accounting perspective, government sponsored nursing home care is a really dumb idea. The government will not only get this euthanasia legislation passed, the average person is going to support this crazy idea. The reason for their support is sobering. Our postmodern society simply does not want these feeble, grouchy, old people disturbing their progressive lifestyles. If you're wondering about those medically dependent cases that need special care – to that I say, hospice. If a local hospice is not medically equipped to handle the medical issues, there is the local hospital, which should only be temporary in order to return our loved one home. When possible, elderly people should die in one of the homes of their children – preferably of the eldest child.

In conclusion of this segment, I understand that in 90% of the elderly cases, this is an impossibility. I understand our society has gone too far and the odds of returning to God's commands are next to impossible. I also have embraced what Jesus said:

" *'Brother will betray brother to death, and a father his child; and children will rise up against parents and cause them to be put to death'* " (Matt.10:21).

I really do understand that we are living in these times. Family honor and respect is so "old school" that we WILL start killing off our loved ones like they are stray dogs and not feel one ounce of guilt because of it. Hard to believe – do you think Jesus is just speaking to homicide via guns and knives? No – it includes abortion, medically assisted termination, euthanasia, and even turning a loved one over to the Antichrist for torture.

To those who are truly listening to what I am trying to communicate, I challenge you to pick up your responsibilities when and wherever possible and do what you can do to support God's design of welfare and family. In those cases where it seems impossible to care for your parent(s) or needy family member, I say, pray. Pray and ask God for a way and then go to your local church and ask for help and guidance as to how they can empower you to support God's idea of family integrated welfare.

CHAPTER 24

GOD GIVES SPECIAL CARE TO THE POOR

When we look closely at God's Word, it really seems like He shows favorites when it comes to the poor and needy.

Poverty creates dependence and dependence begs for special treatment, which is exactly what God gives. Poor people statistically have more faith than wealthy people. What that tells us is that poor people have a special niche about being able to look into the unseen world, which requires an enormous amount of faith. The reason God seems to give special favor to poor people is that poor people classically know that faith is more important than gold and silver. They seem to understand that "without faith it is impossible to please Him" (Heb. 11:6).

I know it is not any fun to view God, or anyone for that matter, as showing favorites over another. Believe me my reader, if anyone has the prerogative to show favoritism – it is the God of the universe.

"Listen, my beloved brethren: did not God choose the poor of this world to be rich in faith and heirs of the kingdom which He promised to those who love Him?" (James 2:5).

This is why we are to listen very closely to the poor. God has chosen and blessed them with a faith that is rare. According to the Holy Scriptures, the poor who love Him are given a special grace when it comes to Salvation and being heirs of the kingdom of God; whereas, with the wealthy and those who strive after it, He tends to be pretty tough. These are not my words, but are God's words.

Our Abba has granted to the poor a special freedom from certain worries, doubts, and fears, which classically plague people who have money or are determined to get it. As a counselor of over 30 years, I can tell you that poor people sleep better at night.

"The sleep of the working man is pleasant, whether he eats little or much; but the full stomach of the rich man does not allow him to sleep" (Eccl. 5:12).

The number one reason why most people do not sleep at night, according to their own answers, is worrying over money problems - either warring over what to do with it or how to get it. As all of us can attest that when we have faith, we have peace; when peace rules, we sleep unencumbered.

One of the questions I have been asked through the years (and hate answering) is: "Why does God allow the wicked to prosper financially?" God allows some evil men to prosper for a season. I believe His purpose seems to be to let them see the emptiness and futility of their constant pursuit of money, wealth, and fame. He's hoping they will one day turn to Him for full-on repentance. He has said that He causes the sun to rise on the evil and the good – no matter their level of prosperity. Personally, I don't think God is so concerned about the "level" of prosperity or poverty.

" 'For He causes His sun to rise on the evil and the good, and sends rain on the righteous and the unrighteous' " (Matt. 5:45).

It is sad for me to say, but most think the "goodness of God" is a sign that they can indulge all the more. The real reason for prosperity is to lead the people into repentance – not a reward of it. God's kindness is not to satisfy our wants or our NEEDS, but rather to usher us into confessing sins for further righteousness.

"Or do you think lightly of the riches of His kindness and tolerance and patience, not knowing that the kindness of God leads you to repentance?" (Rom. 2:4).

The average person uses money to measure God's level of contentment and approval of his life. There is a certain amount of "trouble" that comes with this kind of "stinky thinking." The reason is in how the money is spent.

"Great wealth is in the house of the righteous, but trouble is in the income of the wicked" (Prov. 15:6).

Wicked people typically, if not always, use their funding to spread their base of influence and control. They work their entire lives to make themselves BIGGER than LIFE. When they are gone, all of what they worked tirelessly to obtain, goes into a gold plated casket -- bummer.

"I have seen a wicked, violent man spreading himself like a luxuriant tree in its native soil. Then he passed away, and lo, he was no more; I sought for him, but he could not be found" (Psalm 37:35-36).

I believe we need to look at the other end of the spectrum. Is it possible for God to approve of a dynamic Christian being poor? I know very FEW who do not use financial success as a measuring tool to determine God's level of support for a man's life. Most "Christians" I know actually wonder if God is disciplining the dedicated Christian who is living "hand to mouth." Most of Paul's writings affirm that he had very little money to work with. No, he didn't have some fundraising "campaigners" sustaining his ministry. He certainly learned to be content with wealth and poverty.

God wanted Paul and his coworkers to demonstrate the role and acts of a bondslave; how to endure through all forms of difficulties – while rejoicing in poverty. You see, by doing this, Paul speaks to "85% of the world." Yes, you read it correctly; over 85% of the entire world's population lives "hand to mouth." God wanted Paul to show the majority that we can have nothing and still possess everything. What I just wrote is one of the golden keys to the victorious Christian life.

"But in everything commending ourselves as servants of God, in much endurance, in afflictions, in hardships, in distresses" (2 Cor. 6:4).

"As sorrowful yet always rejoicing, as poor yet making many rich, as having nothing yet possessing all things" (2 Cor. 6:10).

God's children will not only experience poverty from time to time, He purposes to use it to teach His children that He will never leave them or leave them hanging. One who is poor, is usually rich in faith; those who are rich in faith gain the attention of God! Besides, God is not into His children "begging for bread."

"I have been young and now I am old, yet I have not seen the righteous forsaken Or his descendants begging bread" (Psalm 37:25).

Any of you who have traveled to poverty-stricken countries to visit or to serve, know that the faith of those people is rare and is seldom found in an American church. The first time I came back from a trip to Africa, I suffered grief for two weeks attempting to process the difference between American faith and that of the "third world."

CHAPTER 25

STANDARD OF LIVING

Have you ever heard the phrase "that dollar is burning a hole in his pocket?" It used to be a person couldn't wait to spend money that he was about to receive. Then, it was money he "would have." Now, a person can't wait to spend someone else's money, which he has no intention of paying back.

So it is with the level of standard of living that most of us demand. I can remember in my parents' generation, they would have to work their entire lives to buy a house, a used car, and maybe a television. Today, I counsel a generation that typically has a $350,000 house, one car, one van, one motorcycle (his and hers), one television (in each room), and one Jet Ski – all before the age of 27. You think I'm exaggerating? Do your research and what you're going to find is that most young people, married or not, are in debt up to their ears, while tirelessly working to keep the bank from taking their toys.

The average person will raise his standard of living according to how much cash is stuffed in his wallet. Our standard of living should be based upon the contentment of basic essentials. I am afraid that is not the case with most. Since income is becoming more and more unpredictable, these postmodern concepts of money and spending are not cutting it anymore. Whether our income increases or decreases, we need to learn how to manage our lives accordingly.

When God causes our income to increase, it is not for the purpose of spreading out our luxurious living; but rather, to help the needy and poor. It is so easy to lose perspective on this. Usually what happens is that God will increase our base and we make the sinful mistake of setting our focus on the increase. God clearly warns us of this.

"Do not trust in oppression and do not vainly hope in robbery; if riches increase, do not set your heart upon them" (Psalm 62:10).

Trusting in oppression? Do not vainly hope in robbery? Just by a mere glance, these two warnings seem a bit odd. The Hebrew word there for "oppression" is "osheq," which means "fraud or unjust gain." The Hebrew word for "vainly" in this passage is "habal," which means "being led astray." Finally, the Hebrew word of "robbery" is "gazel," which means "plunder or gain of others." When we put the three of these meanings together, we get this:

Do not trust in fraud or unjust gain and do not be led astray by your hope in the profits of others.

With that being said, we need to contemplate on what it means to "trust in fraud and unjust gain." Any form of financial gain, which is not 100% reliance on God and His divine will, is fraud. Those who are captured by the deception that oppressing others is a means of financial gain will automatically be lead astray to rob others. They will use the gain of others to secure their financial portfolios. That is how simple this is.

GAMBLING: Have you ever really taken the time to analyze the true definition of gambling? The original meaning is "investing money with the hope of making money on other people's losses." But if we look at the true nature behind gambling, we will see a clear violation of Psalm 62:10. Typically, when one person wins, another is oppressed (loses). We might say that this is the point of "gambling." Most people relate gambling to cards, slot machines, and poker. Even by the definition in most dictionaries, the truth of the matter is gambling encompasses insurance companies, the stock market, sports' pools, making money off of foreclosures and bankruptcy, and even, bingo. The general principle is based upon robbery. Instead of using our funding to help those who are getting ready to lose their home, cars, etc., gambling takes advantage of those losses. This is why God is so against it!

So – is it wrong for Christians to have wealth? No, but it is wrong to use that wealth to feed off of the losses of an oppressed person. God is quick to correct and discipline those who heap up riches for themselves.

"Surely every man walks about as a phantom (secret one); surely they make an uproar for nothing; He amasses (stores up) riches and does not know who will gather them" (Psalm 39:6, parentheses mine).

It is so easy for those of wealth to become puffed up and proud. When this happens, they start looking at their accumulation of wealth like it is a child. They start caring for and babysitting their money, more than caring for people. This is not always the case, but it is most common. The greatest violation is to fall into the temptation of switching the focus from God to the amasses.

"Instruct those who are rich in this present world not to be conceited or to fix their hope on the uncertainty of riches, but on God, who richly supplies us with all things to enjoy" (1 Tim. 6:17).

Rich people tend to love money. In most cases, this IS why they are rich. He who loves riches will ultimately hate those who try to take it from them: government, family, friends, investors, or the world in general. The positive aspect of a godly person having riches is that he gives God the glory for the wealth and the reason for having it. He understands it is God who is able to make all grace abound toward him. If God decided to take it all away, he would continue to consider being sufficient in all things. Why? Because he is continuing to abound in good works – helping the poor.

"And God is able to make all grace abound to you, so that always having all sufficiency in everything, you may have an abundance for every good deed" (2 Cor. 9:8).

The bottom line is simple. When God increases your wealth, don't increase your standard of living. First, look around to see who or what God is wanting you to help with that extra cash. If He continues to increase your wealth, be extra careful about raising that standard of living. Work to live as if you are hand to mouth, so you can help those who do. Not being content with what you have is at the base of all temptations. Realize and appropriate what God has given you - everything you need for your present standard of living. Struggling with discontentment starts the downward cycle of spiritual, emotional, and financial bankruptcy.

CHAPTER 26

HUMBLY SUFFERING NEED

The proper and most honorable way to find out someone's true character is by suddenly taking something away from him. The perfect way to find out an individual's pride level is by giving him something with great value. The way we find out if a person can be trusted with things of GREATER value is by entrusting something of little value.

Did you know that a pattern (cycle) can be found in the Scriptures regarding riches and poverty? It is true! God normally does not view riches or poverty as a permanent condition in the life of an individual, family, or even a nation. Notice that I said, "normally."

Christ Himself was and is an incredibly wealthy man! The wealth He had while walking the face of the earth could not be measured by man. Think about it – a man, who literally owned the entire universe and then some, humbled Himself to suffer the need of poverty - being poor.

"For you know the grace of our Lord Jesus Christ, that though He was rich, yet for your sake He became poor, so that you through His poverty might become rich" (2 Cor. 8:9).

I saw a television show recently showing a millionaire pretending to be a person with a below average to average income. The mission was to "hit the streets" to visit the lowly and the organizations that serve them. At the end of the show, the millionaire would reveal his true identity and offer the organizations, which authentically "deserved" it, a large sum of cash. At first I thought, "Another reality show." But after watching it, I quickly realized this concept is biblically accurate. In all actuality, that is what Christ did! He (Christ) is the literal Son of the Patriarch of the universe, the wealthiest being in the whole universe and beyond. He was sent to humble Himself by suffering the need. During His short stay on this earth, He could have made every impoverished or needy person whom He came into contact with RICH by one spoken word; but, He didn't. Instead, He suffered with and tested each of them, to see whose faith would be enhanced and who was deserving of true riches, the kind that never rusts.

People who have learned to be content with being both rich and poor, full and hungry, quenched and thirsty, are the ones who will be honored and blessed with the riches found only in heaven (Phil. 4:11-12).

How was it that Christ, being the richest of eternity, was able to come to earth, humble Himself, and become one of the lowly? The key is "contentment." The Greek word for "contentment" is "autarkes," which means "to know one's place." Any person who knows one's place in life is able to be at peace with humble circumstances. Anyone who does not know his place in eternity is NOT able to humble himself. This is why God obligates Himself to humble others. A content person is able to renounce all desire and want for the sake of another person's gain; BUT, only with the power of Christ flowing in and through him.

Where do you stand in the checklist of humbly accepting suffer?

✓	Wealth and Success	✓	Poverty and Suffering
	I am grateful for the provisions I have.		I am able to be silent about my needs when there is no provision available.
	I enjoy an abundance of food and clothing.		I know how to endure hunger, a lack of clothing, and even a lack of shelter.
	I joyfully pass on honor to the Lord when others lift me up and praise me for my efforts.		I accept rejection, neglect, embarrassment, and persecution when allowed by God.
	I make use of my material things to better the lives of the lowly.		When I am lowly, I have learned to get along without material things and to be joyful about it.
	I enjoy the physical comforts available to me without feeling		I endure and accept the fact that physical comforts in life

	guilt.		are temporary and not to be counted on as the norm.
	Even though all my material needs are being met, I still practice the art of receiving help from others.		When others are not around, or refuse to offer help, I am still content with not receiving. I have learned to draw upon the resources of Christ.
	I am well content and pleased when my outward circumstances don't work out according to my own desires, wealth, and plans.		I have learned to refuse dependence upon outward circumstances.
	I am not embarrassed by my wealth and comforts in life.		To be homeless and face death due to no funding is a scary idea; but I have embraced the possibility as God's sovereign hand.
	I am willing to lose it all for the sake of Christ.		I am willing to become rich for the sake of Christ.

How did you do? Not so good? No worries – most of us don't. Sordid gain carries a great deal of trouble with it. It puffs us up and causes us to be blinded to the reality of God's desire to humble us with the needy. We all suffer with this. Poverty is such a blessing and there are great rewards connected to those who have learned to endure by it. A family that learns to love, when they have only bread to eat, is richer than the neighbor who has strife and a fattened cow spread across their family dining room table.

The cool thing about all this conviction stuff is: God's kindness leads us to repentance. If you're one of those who are being convicted, consider it as a gentle nudge to lead you to the feet of Jesus to repent.

God takes every Christian through a horrid time of discipline and pruning to increase his faith and move him to being fruitful in all things. Overall, He is causing us to be a reflection of the very life and face of Jesus Christ.

CHAPTER 27

ADVERTISEMENT JUNKY

Did you know that advertisements rarely work unless they appeal to an addiction? The question would then be, "What is an addiction?" I wish I could give you more of a glorified definition than this, but it is "an additive to one's life." I know, we are used to hearing that it is some substance that actually causes a person's body to be dependent upon it. The truth is that an addiction adds something to one's life that is not needed.

One of the most used Scriptures in my counseling sessions is 1 John 2:15-16. It says:

"Do not love the world nor the things in the world. If anyone loves the world, the love of the Father is not in him. For all that is in the world, the lust of the flesh and the lust of the eyes and the boastful pride of life, is not from the Father, but is from the world" (1 John 2:15-16).

God is giving us a clear warning about loving the world or things in the world. In fact, He is so strong in this passage that He leaves us with the evidence that those who do love the world and its possessions do not have the love of the Heavenly Father in them. Ouch! That hurts.

People who love the world are friends with the world. Those who are friends with the world put themselves in a hostile position before the living God. People who work to be friends with the world's concepts, its people, or systems, make themselves a literal enemy of God. I know what you're thinking, "You thought we were supposed to be friends with the unsaved in order for them to become saved, right?" Wrong. God does tell us to "befriend" our enemies, strangers, and even people we know for the purpose of leading them to Christ; but being friends means an exchange of identity or becoming familiar (family). This type of "friendship" is oneness. Those who become one with the world soon realize how wrong it is to become a friend with those outside of the family of God.

"You adulteresses, do you not know that friendship with the world is hostility toward God? Therefore whoever wishes to be a friend of the world makes himself an enemy of God" (James 4:4).

Advertisements appeal to our flesh. It is our flesh that is a graven mirror to the face of Satan and this world is his temporary dwelling place. God wants us to hate our flesh and never become friends with it. As usual, no one says it better than Jesus:

" *'He who loves his life loses it, and he who hates his life in this world will keep it to life eternal' "* (John 12:25).

Self-love is not a healthy action. When Jesus says "he who loves his life loses it," He is obviously showing us the error in "learning to love yourself." The truth of the matter is that God commands us to "hate" ourselves in order to be able to embrace eternal life. Since Satan knows this to be true, he works to get people to "learn to love themselves." His goal is to set a mark of "perfection" in which the majority of human life will fall short. Once this happens, the human will do just about anything to measure up to that mark (plastic surgery, implants, lifts, reductions, dyes, tanning, weight loss, weight gain, buffeting the body, exercise, and the list only goes on from there). Satan is quick to project a "perfect" image that 90% of the world cannot measure up to – even if they had plastic surgery to reach their goal. Satan is the craftiest, or most subtle, created being in all of creation (Gen. 3:1). One of the primary ways he accomplishes this deception is through advertisements.

Here is how he does it. He goes out into the world and recruits those "perfect" model types (who usually got that way through drugs and anorexia) and places them front and center on a billboard. He places some crazed message about how if you buy their product, "You, too, can look like Miss Anorexia." And you know what? It works. People start picking up those cell phones and order products that will only enhance the way they already look.

Advertisements would never work if the boundary lines of authority were at work in the lives of the people. Satan always goes from the bottom up! His little plan of going to Eve first was not by accident – it was strategically planned. Why didn't Satan go to Adam first? Because he knew his advertisement would not sell him. Adam knew he was under the authority of God directly and Satan knew Eve was indirectly under the authority of God through Adam. This, in Satan's eyes, was the perfect avenue to do his little billboard thing, which is exactly what he did. He took an already perfect image and added to it (remember our definition of addiction). This became the first advertisement gimmick to man and beast. He has not stopped using this technique to this very day. He will always go from the bottom up. If he can continue to cause a rebellion to authority figures, he can continue to appeal to fleshing friendships through his advertisements.

Imagine this for a moment. If every purchase had to be cleared for approval by an authority figure, how many advertisements of Satan would actually make the sell? Not many, my dear reader. If Eve would have taken the "apple" over to Adam and asked him if she should eat the apple from the "forbidden tree," I am fairly certain the answer would have been – NO. Satan has formed an almost flawless system of control and he isn't about to change his manipulative ways anytime soon. Seductive advertisements typically encourage us to ignore, question, or come against those principles that are designed to protect us.

Like in the garden, advertisements cause us to focus on that "one thing," which will make us look, feel, or be more successful. In reality, the opposite usually happens and we become in debt over this "life changing" product. Remember when Satan said to Eve, "You shall not surely die" (Gen. 3:4). Well, he was right - kind of. Even though she did not die physically right there on the spot; spiritually, she died instantly. It was from this covert twisted truth that Satan was able to cause his advertisement to sell her. God clearly warned Adam and Eve that if they ate from the Tree of Knowledge they would die, but the two of them continued to eat. Satan was counting on Adam and Eve not "getting it" right away. It was a "good gamble" on Satan's part, because it worked! It all started by an advertisement to Eve, then an advertisement from Eve to Adam, and from Adam to his soul. Most people tend to believe the "results" they see on the billboard, not in the bottle (product). Most advertisements are based on the assumed benefits and not on the hard facts. A good example of this is in medicines that have lists of side effects longer than the complaints. Some even have side effects like "suicidal ideations," "depression," and "feelings of rage" - and they still sell a billion of them. People go for assumed benefits, NOT facts. That is the power of advertisements.

ADS AROUSE DISCONTENTMENT: An advertisement would not be a good ad unless it left us feeling discontent. Discontentment is at the base of all effective ads. The company wants us to feel as if something is missing in our life if we don't have its product. This trick is as old as human life. Satan used the same tactic on Eve. He convinced her that she was missing out of something really important for her happiness. The truth being said, God had already blessed her with the fullness of joy. Discontentment cannot be birthed unless the person has a feeling that more can fit into his bags of happiness. With that said, Satan works diligently to drain us of contentment. Once he does that – its billboard time.

ADS PROMOTE INDEPENDENCE: Genesis 3:5 reveals to us that Satan said "Ye shall be as gods" (KJV). Wow! Now that is an ad. Be a god. How cool is that? As you have already guessed, Eve (and Adam) bought that one "hook, line, and sinker." One of the greatest temptations to mankind is being our own boss, or better yet, god - to answer to no one. Well, how better could it get? True independence is death and Satan worked really hard to cover that little tidbit in his dialogue with Eve. As soon as Eve fell to this lie, she moved from being under God's pinion to being a woman of opinion, which translates as "being your own pinion."

ADS PROMOTE HOARDING: Have you ever taken the time to get to know a hoarder? They will tell you that the majority of their piles are a result of being hooked by an ad – a bargain. Not all those who are addicted to ads hoard. But those who do will reveal that it is usually from a loss of a loved one: someone died, divorced, or ran off on them. From that loss, the appeals and pull of the ads begin to be more convincing than ever before. They buy and store "stuff" around them – all in an effort to fill the empty space that reminds them of their empty lives. Hoarders are a loud and visual picture of what Satan's world of advertisements can do.

The televised version of hoarders is not the true picture of this problem. For example: In America, more than any other country in the world, people spend their hard earned money on renting "self-storage" units to neatly hide their hoarding. Not all hoarders pile it around them by filling their living space. Most, in fact, do it in such an organized fashion that the world rarely sees their nasty habit. Yes, it is one of the most selfish acts of man; but in truth, it is a real addictive problem for many.

ADS DEMAND HUMAN REASONING: There is a big difference between human reason and God reason. Satan only appeals to human logic – NEVER God's logic. He (Satan) would prefer us to choose between good and evil according to our own minds (1 John 4:1). As long as this human understanding thing is ruling our hearts, the ads will continue to appeal to us. As soon as we switch to God's logic and reason (His Word), the Satanic ads cease from working.

BUT, I NEED IT: This is probably the worst one in the bunch. The enemy not only appeals to our wants; but he appeals even more to our needs, food, clothing, water, shelter, and companionship. If he can successfully move us from trusting God for our daily bread to ourselves, then again, the ad will do its job. This is the enemy's way of allowing the buyer to justify his impulsive buying. Have you ever seen an ad that says "Don't buy this product unless God tells you to" or "Don't buy this dress unless your husband approves of it"? – I don't think so! Half the fun of buying impulsively is lying about it – at least that is what I'm told.

PLEASANT TO THE EYE: I think when Satan was finished with his advertisement, Eve saw the food was good to eat (pleasant to the eye) and would make her wise, so she bought the product. That is the point about this ad stuff: If it doesn't capture the eye, then what is the point? Satan was right there when He (God) created Adam and formed Eve. He knows that the "eye is the window to the soul" and due to this truth, the eye must be used in order to get the bite. Eve biting into that fruit is for us, purchasing the product. Times have not changed. The same old same old is the same old Satan. His tricks have not changed AT ALL.

The bottom line is that the enemy is working himself to the bone to get us to find fulfillment in all the wrong places. Anything, any place, or any person aside from God will work for him. He doesn't care about the wrinkle cream, the new car, or even the ad for that favored Bible school. What he really cares about is stopping God's people (or any person) from depending on His voice and His voice alone. Idolatry is one of Satan's favorite hobbies. He loves getting others to depend on people, places, and things that have nothing to do with God. For God and Satan both know that when people bow down and worship an idol, their faces are directed toward him (Satan).

Advertisements are needed and key in keeping and maintaining a person's bondage to debt. For without all these fancy ads, we probably would not have debt. I am in search for the dollar figure spent worldwide on advertisements last year. I haven't found the amount yet, but I have a feeling that if I did, there probably would be enough money to feed the hungry and clothe the naked for many years to come.

Are all forms of advertisements bad or "of the devil?" No, they are not; but even a good and integral ad can create bondage. My challenge for each of us is not to figure out the "evil" ads versus the "good." Rather, we need to put our focus on living out the biblical guidelines of God's miraculous plan of economy and learn ways to resist sales.

CHAPTER 28

RESTING SALES AND BARGAINS

Recently, my wife and I stumbled onto a television show called Extreme Couponing. Since we are avid promoters of using coupons, we thought we might take this show in. To no surprise, we found a list of people, primarily women, who were addicted to a sale or a bargain. They all used the excuse that if it is free or an "extreme" savings, one should buy it. In one case in point, a lady had a three-year-supply of diapers, but no children. Her stated reasoning was, "If and when I have children." These people have every corner of their homes and garages packed with stuff they probably will never use. In reality, these people are "organized hoarders."

As I was watching this show, I was reminded of something Jesus said.

"Then He said to them, 'Beware, and be on your guard against every form of greed; for not even when one has an abundance does his life consist of his possessions' " (Luke 12:15).

Generically speaking, material possessions hinder our ability to embrace the richness of Jesus Christ. This is why we must be willing to experience the loss of all things and even count them as worthless, in order to gain a much larger understanding of our Husband. It is through our riches in Christ that we are able to totally enjoy the hand of the Lord in supernatural provision.

"The naive believes everything, but the sensible man considers his steps" (Prov. 14:15).

The word "naïve" in the Hebrew is "pethiy," which means "seducible." The word "sensible" in the Hebrew is "arum," which means "prudent" or "making use of senses." With this insight, we can now read the verse in this way:

"The seducible believes everything, but the man who relies upon his senses, considers his steps."

Salesmen in the marketplace are counting on the "seducible" to believe everything told to them in their ads. The logic is simple! The salespeople know that less that 10% of people are the "sensible" types; therefore, they really don't care about the "organized hoarders." To be successful, the sales representatives point out the positive aspects of their products, while they downplay the negative. They leave it to the buyer to search out the negative, which is rarely done. What does that mean for the company? It means cash in their pockets. Plus, there is a marketing secret that few know; the FREE, or highly discounted, items are what the corporate world calls "junk products." These are items that are cheap to make, are overstocked, or are simply "junk." The loss margin is so low, they don't care if the 10% get these items FREE or next to nothing. This is why these "organized hoarders" will have 106 cans of sodium-enriched, trans-fatted, hydrogenated junk on their shelves. How often do we find these kinds of deals on organic and natural products? We don't. It is actually one of the oldest "tricks" in the trade.

"Lying lips are an abomination to the LORD, but those who deal faithfully are His delight" (Prov. 12:22).

How many sales or corporate representatives would you say are lying? A better question would be - how many sales representatives aren't lying? The goal of most companies is to create discontentment in our souls. This is done by somehow making us think that what we have isn't "good enough" anymore or what we do have is outdated or inadequate. Companies try to convince us that if we don't have their product, it will stunt our happiness or success. In reality, God is telling us to enjoy our present possessions. He wants us to remember that He has entrusted us with a certain level of material pleasure, in order to test us in our stewardship.

"A prudent man sees evil and hides himself, the naive proceed and pay the penalty" (Prov. 27:12).

Yes, you read that correctly. A wise man will actually run and hide when he sees seducible evil, which will lure him away from the way of the Lord. Whereas, the "seducible" (naïve) keep moving toward the cash register to pay the penalty.

Each year, millions of people buy into "get rich quick" schemes. We used to call them "fraudulent swindlers." Today, we call them "multilevel marketers" or "financial campaigns." It is nothing more or less than clever schemes to take our money in exchange for worthless ideas or products - usually stuff that barely lasts a year or turns to waste matter in a day. People who live off of these "get rich quick" ideas typically feed off feelings of inferiority, guilt, greed, and other lustful passions buried within the souls of their victims. Junk salesmen usually target independent people who only answer to themselves. Salespeople know that authority figures are the protective wall between them and their victims. If a woman said, "This all sounds great, but I will need to talk with my husband/father about this before making a decision" – well, that simply would stop them dead in their tracks. This is also why we find Satan doing everything within his means to reduce authority figures to nothing.

THE BAIT: If you have ever gone fishing or hunting, you know that there are four primary elements needed to catch your prey: the bait, the hook, the distraction, and the bite. Most advertisers work off of the fact that we have secret dreams lying dormant and waiting to be fulfilled. Their job is to find the right kind of bait to draw us to the hook. This "draw" usually involves some type of perceived "need" in our life. Once they are able to appeal to this perceived need, they are fairly certain we are going to bite into the hook.

THE HOOK: The success of an effective salesperson or advertisement is achieved not only by having the right kind of bait, but also the perfect hook. The advertisement hook involves confessions, testimonies, or statements that penetrate the hidden motives, or those secret dreams, hidden within our flesh. One of the greatest appeals is "to get something for nothing." Nothing is sweeter to a deal lover than to get something that someone else has to pay for. The development of the "sharp hook" is a known and well-researched variable in its ability to get the job done.

Those of you who fish, understand the importance of "planting the hook." You watch the bobber (statistics), you feel the tugging, and in that perfect moment of setting the hook, you pull like the dickens. Bam, you caught one!

THE PLANT: Swindlers use advertisements in a selfish way. They often work in teams and will strategically place others around us (the shopper), in order to create some excitement. Actors are hired to ACT like real customers who are satisfied with their product. This is what we call "planting the hook." The only thing real about these paid testimonies is their makeup. The rest is as fake as their smiles. These compensated testimonials are paid to do one thing – to keep our eyes on the bait, so the company can set the hook.

THE BITE: Aha - the moment the company has been waiting for. During the phase of the bite, the fish really doesn't do much of the work, the fisherman does. It works the same way with advertisements. Once the individual gets to the point of having the hook in his mouth, odds are that he will buy!

How do we stop this horrid cycle? It's pretty easy. Decide to seek counsel before purchasing anything over $50. This is even easier for a married woman; just wait for the setting of the hook and then say, "I don't make these kinds of decisions without permission from my husband." Single gals may wish to say, "I don't make these kinds of decisions without permission from my father." Males may say the same thing, but use the term father or counsel. Done!

Was that too easy? Of course it was. This is why most swindling types of salespeople are hoping we have an authority problem. Did you hear what I just said? These companies are desperately hoping we have a real attitude about authority figures. They know if we use the simple approach spelled out above, the deal is dead!

The only salvation to protect ourselves against swindling salespeople and advertisements is to: commit to following scriptural principles, seek counsel from authority figures, and lean upon the Holy Spirit within us. This I will promise you - the Holy Spirit will never lead us into debt!

CHAPTER 29

THE SUPPER SAVER

Have you ever shopped with someone who is an extreme super saver? I do every week – my wife. She has simply mastered the art of how to get the best buy possible. Working alongside someone like this is either completely annoying or fascinating.

VALUE: I think the reason my wife is able to do this is because she understands the value of money, what it is for, and how God wants her to make use of it. Usually, value is understood by comparing it to something else.

For example: You and your family decide to go out to eat. After looking at the menu, you quickly do the numbers in your head and realize you are about to spend your miscellaneous food AND gas money. You might decide to go to a fast-food place instead.

The problem is that very few people do comparisons like this and thus, spend their survival money. Just yesterday, I heard my wife say that she is not going to buy our weekly groceries while I am away on a weeklong trip, so that she can put the food money toward the upcoming Homeschool Convention. That is value comparison at its best.

COST COMPARISON: I can't tell you how many times I have picked up an item thinking I had picked the best price on the shelf, when my wife pipes up with, "Wait, I don't have a coupon for that." Price comparison involves more than just selecting the best marked sale item off the shelf. It involves going to the right store, using the best coupons, going on double coupon day, choosing quantity with quality, and deciding not to be led by impulse. There is a great feeling that comes over a person when working at cost comparison and winning. I hope you understand what I am trying to say here. We do not advocate buying junk. If we're going to spend our money, we should spend it on quality and quantity. Most "deals" in the stores are on junk items. That does not mean we should use that supersized coupon to buy that hydrogenated bag of toxic waste. We ought to spend our hard earned money on quality with a discount.

PERCENTAGES VERSUS CENTS: My wife tells me that one of the "tricks of the trade" is to calculate the savings by percentages, not by cents. Yes, that's correct - by percentage. It is one thing to save a few cents on a can of beans; but if we can save that percentage on our entire food bill, now we have really saved. This is what they are doing on those extreme coupon shows on television. They are not interested in how much they save on the toothpaste per box. They're more interested in walking away from the cash register, while hearing the cashier say, "You have saved 90% on your shopping today." These people understand the principle of "percentage versus cents."

How does this work on an item-by-item basis? Before we get to the cash register, or even at home, we write on the coupon what percentage will be saved by using that coupon. If the coupon does not meet our standard of savings – WE DON'T BUY IT. If you believe you really must have that item, well, like I tell my kids, "If you really have to go, go ahead and use that dirty bathroom, BUT do it quickly."

" 'He who is faithful in a very little thing is faithful also in much; and he who is unrighteous in a very little thing is unrighteous also in much' " (Luke 16:10).

NEVER SHOP BY CREDIT OR DEBIT: Ouch, did I have to say that? This is the number one reason many shoppers get into so much trouble. The simple system of banking our money before we spend it is a wise one. Getting the best buy requires carefully guarding and accounting for the money we have budgeted for that shopping event. When we get paid, we should consider going into the bank and asking for cash back to place in the envelopes marked with specific categories ("food money," "spending," "gas," etc.). When it comes to grocery shopping, we must work from that particular envelope. If our list doesn't match the amount we have to spend, we need to find some coupons or reduce the list. It is that simple. We should never go into the store thinking we can use our credit card to pay the bill, instead of only using what's in the "food envelope." First of all, few do what they say when it comes to money. Secondly, we should rarely buy things on credit. What about that debit card? If we are disciplined enough to occasionally use that debit card to pay for our groceries and put the food money back into the bank by the next day, then go right ahead. How many do you think do that? You guessed it – few.

CASH AND CARRY: Embracing the above principle requires the ownership of this principle. All shoppers need to get into the habit of doing much of their purchases with cash, not checks or debit cards. I am not saying that using a checkbook or a debit card is a sin. I am saying that it is a bad practice to get into. Setting cash aside for purchases helps us plan, account, and conduct value shopping. By using paper (checks) or plastic (debit cards), it is so difficult to see the value slip out of our fingers. When we use cash – well -- no one likes to part with cash. It is proven that doing "cash and carry" either forces stewardship or leaves the buyer with holes in his pockets. For those whose cash tends to burn holes in their pockets, to that I say, "Get help!"

DECIDE BEFORE YOU BUY: Those who have a list before going into the store know how much they will spend, know exactly what they will spend their money on, and will usually leave the store feeling pretty good. It is also proven that those who come into the store with a file of product advertisements, compared pricing, and a list marked with the items they intend to buy are less apt to have sales clerks apply pressure on them. The reason for this is the sales reps know these people have done their homework and will not be quick to fall into their snare.

SET YOUR MIND ON THE LIST – NOT THE BALANCE: Most people buy according to how much they have in their account. They play this game of running the account to the edge as close as they can without "bouncing" (overdrawing) their account. This really is a nasty habit to get into. Actually, it is a confession on how they tend to run their spiritual lives. If we go shopping with "envelope money," this will never happen. We will have predetermined to spend according to our list and envelope, not our bank account. When people shop without lists or cash, they tend to look to the bank instead of the list.

THE TAG VERSUS THE PRODUCT: I am going to share with you a profound, but simple technique that will save you thousands of dollars. Always look at the price tag before investing a single minute into looking at the product. All sales schools train sales representatives with the opposite in mind. They want us caught up in the shiny chrome and fresh smelling leather before we ask how much the little beauty is.

Here is how to do it. If a new vacuum cleaner is on your list, cash is in the pocket, and the file papers are in hand – then, you are ready. Walk into the department/store boldly, as if you have already found what you are going to buy. Walk up to the item and look at the price tag. About that time, the sales representative will be on your tail. They will ask if they can help you. You say, "No, I have already found what I am looking for and it is overpriced." They will take your bait and now you become the fisherman. Open your file and show the clerk what you want and the maximum price you are willing to pay. If they say that price is impossible to beat, or match, then walk away. Most clerks play this game to determine their level of commission. Oftentimes, stores will have hidden policies giving the sales people permission to come back with, "Let me talk to my manager." What they are really saying is, "I will be back with our bottom line." If this store does not beat or match this price, leave at once. No more shopping or you could be tempted to go back.

COUNT THE COST: When putting our shopping lists together, it is important we actually count the full cost of the spending spree. While sitting down to plan for the shopping trip, list out the store's regular price, the sale price, tax, and any other fees that might come with the purchase.

Knowing the full price before heading out to the store is a common "trick of the trade" for healthy shoppers. Keep in mind that Satan's plan is to trip us up once we get into the store, by making use of every venue of lust he can muster. If we have a plan and have already decided NOT to deviate from it, we are probably going to pass the test.

PRICING QUANTITY BUYING: Another trick my wife taught me is that the economy size is not always the best buy. It is true that most things can be bought in economy size and we can get more for our buck, but we have to watch this trick very carefully.

Store marketers like to play this game because most of the time, it works. Many times, items are actually more expensive per ounce or pound. If the store does not provide the unit price (most state laws require it now), we will have to calculate it. In order to figure out the unit price, divide the cost by the number of ounces. It is wisest to shop by unit price when it comes to quantity buying.

These are simple things to remember when it comes to shopping day. Oh – don't forget to total everything before getting into the checkout line (my wife and I do it as we shop). And ladies, never send your husband out shopping unless he has been trained in the do's and don'ts of proper shopping – or else he might come home with that new flat screen.

CHAPTER 30

BEING HELD IN ACCOUNT

"Everything was numbered and weighed, and all the weight was recorded at that time" (Ezra 8:34).

"In this case, moreover, it is required of stewards that one be found trustworthy" (1 Cor. 4:2).

If you're like most people, you probably hate paperwork. Recordkeeping is simply a "pain" in a world that is filled with business. I can tell you this; those who do keep adequate records are admitting to understanding the value and purpose of money. Recordkeeping is primarily for the master: a boss, husband, government, or board of directors. It also allows us to visually see exactly what God has entrusted to us.

A record, or accounting, system is the basis for a means in which others, primarily God, can hold us accountable for the provisions entrusted to us by Him. Those who seek and strive to be rich and increase in their goods, while avoiding accountability, tend to become either emergent or lukewarm.

" *'So because you are lukewarm, and neither hot nor cold, I will spit you out of My mouth. Because you say, "I am rich, and have become wealthy, and have need of nothing," and you do not know that you are wretched and miserable and poor and blind and naked'* " (Rev. 3:16-17).

Most of us consider our personal financial status to be private and no one's business but our own. The truth of the matter is – that is not true. All Christians should be willing to have their entire lives be an open book, including their finances. Using what God has entrusted to us involves using all of the resources God has given (spiritually, psychologically, and financially), according to His divine PURPOSES.

Which do you think Christ would consider more valuable: a million dollars safely invested in a secure stock or a cup of cold water to a thirsty soul? If you think like I do, your mind might conclude that we could take the million and quench the thirst of thousands. But the real to life answer is Christ would rather we give the one cup of water. The question is: "When is the man thirsty?"

"Your gold and your silver have rusted; and their rust will be a witness against you and will consume your flesh like fire. It is in the last days that you have stored up your treasure!" (James 5:3).

God's original design of multiplying money is by trading, buying, or selling – not by stocks and bonds (inflation). In fact, inflationary wealth is a form of stealing. When there is no means to make money off of people's losses (stocks/bonds), God's people are more apt to increase their wealth through earnings and productivity, resourcefulness, and let's not forget – savings.

Many use the parable Jesus told in Matthew 13 as a reason for making money off of other people's losses (stocks/bonds).

" *'The kingdom of heaven is like a treasure hidden in the field, which a man found and hid again; and from joy over it he goes and sells all that he has and buys that field. Again, the kingdom of heaven is like a merchant seeking fine pearls, and upon finding one pearl of great value, he went and sold all that he had and bought it'* " (Matt. 13:44-46).

I can't tell you how many times I have had someone use this passage as a reason to sell everything they have to invest in a stock that will "double" or even "triple" their investment. I am always amazed at how we humans turn Jesus' examples into depraved concepts in which to prosper ourselves. The message in these parables (the hidden treasure in the field and the pearl of great price) is in the unfolding of their spiritual value. If properly translated, they would read this way:

The kingdom of heaven is the Great Pearl hidden to the eyes of man, and if a man finds this Pearl of Great Price, Jesus Christ, he will sell everything he has, give it to the poor, and give his life to Christ.

If you remember, this is the very thing Jesus required of the rich man in Matt. 19:21, "Jesus said to him, 'If you wish to be complete, go and sell your possessions and give to the poor, and you will have treasure in heaven; and come, follow Me.' "

The key in these stories is that the wise money manager sold what he had and purchased something of FAR greater value. The real question always comes back to, "What is of the greatest value?" When we lose sight of this, we start stockpiling worthless things. Some even rent storage units to hold all their treasures. A mentor once told me, "If you haven't used it in the past year - sell, trade, or give it away." Good advice.

The majority of the "Christian Church" populous today is emergent/lukewarm – that is for certain. As I watch the church lose its salt in our postmodern world, I am reminded of what Jesus said to the church of Laodicea:

" 'I advise you to buy from Me gold refined by fire so that you may become rich, and white garments so that you may clothe yourself, and that the shame of your nakedness will not be revealed; and eye salve to anoint your eyes so that you may see ' " (Rev. 3:18).

The fact is that life requires trading, selling, or giving things away of lesser value, for things that our hearts consider to be of greater value - even if it is a smile on someone's face. It really becomes difficult, in many cases impossible, to live like this if we do not keep good records of the stuff we have. Yes, I am advocating that people inventory ALL their stuff – junk and valuables. This way if someone states a need, walk over to that file, read down the list to find the item of need, read where the item is stored, and go get it. How does one function being this organized? Simple - when "decluttering," bring the file folder with you. On the inventory sheets inside the folder, include two columns: the item name and where it is stored. Also, consider adding a third column: the date the item was stored. Some folks like to do this with freezer items or whatever tickles their fancy.

ACCOUNTING FOR THINGS: People who can account for all their stuff are actually able to live within their means more than those who live on the edge of impulsivity. One of the most practical ideas is purchasing pre-purchased stuff. Did you know that 30% of all unnecessary purchases are already stuffed in a cubbyhole somewhere at home? People are either too lazy or they simply do not have adequate records of locating that "needed" item. Once at the store, they deceive themselves into thinking a newer one will better serve them. It used to be that people were too proud to use pre-owned stuff. Now, most don't even want to use their own pre-owned stuff; everything must be new. This is why manufacturers purposely make things to last a maximum of one year. They have the same stats I have.

MAKING A PLAN: God said to make a plan and He will come and direct our steps. So when I look at the average person who comes into my office for help and see how out of order their lives are, I quickly see how much of their lives are not managed by God.

"The mind of man plans his way, But the LORD directs his steps" (Prov. 16:9).

It doesn't matter if it is God or man, managers cannot direct the steps of their people if there is no pathway. Wise people make plans, count the cost, and submit the plan to the boss (God). Fools spontaneously walk and don't bother making a path. The only path they make is the one behind them. These people call themselves ungifted in the area of organization. Actually, that is an excuse and they know it. People perish without a plan!

It is difficult for most people to realize that when they make a plan and submit it to God, He has the provisions and sufficient funds to support the plan in ways the human cannot. The general rule is that if there are not sufficient funds and resources for a plan, then the wise steward should not move forward with the project – at least at that time. Spontaneous and unplanned people know this deep down inside and this is why they just "jump in." This is also why those of us who struggle with being impulsively spontaneous get mocked!

" 'For which one of you, when he wants to build a tower, does not first sit down and calculate the cost to see if he has enough to complete it? Otherwise, when he has laid a foundation and is not able to finish, all who observe it begin to ridicule him, saying, "This man began to build and was not able to finish" ' " (Luke 14:28-30).

CHAPTER 31

MONEY MATTERS TO GOD

One of the verses that shake my foundation more than most is found in Romans 14:

"So then each one of us will give an account of himself to God" (Rom. 14:12).

Ouch, that "give an account" phrase is what really hurts. Most of us go through our day just living life according to our own timetable and predetermined way. Let's face it; having an accounting system that backs and supports our financial dealings is laborious and time-consuming. We typically don't believe we have enough energy or time. Having an adequate accounting system is both living proof and a subtle confession. We believe that someday we will be held in account for how we managed what was entrusted to us.

Did you know that God has an accounting department and system? It is true! Check this out:

"Now the rest of the acts of Jehoshaphat, first to last, behold, they are written in the annals of Jehu the son of Hanani, which is recorded in the Book of the Kings of Israel" (2 Chron. 20:34).

"May they be blotted out of the book of life And may they not be recorded with the righteous" (Psalm 69:28).

"It will come about that he who is left in Zion and remains in Jerusalem will be called holy--everyone who is recorded for life in Jerusalem" (Isa. 4:3).

" 'Nevertheless do not rejoice in this, that the spirits are subject to you, but rejoice that your names are recorded in heaven' " (Luke 10:20).

"For as many as are of the works of the Law are under a curse; for it is written, 'CURSED IS EVERYONE WHO DOES NOT ABIDE BY ALL THINGS

WRITTEN IN THE BOOK OF THE LAW, TO PERFORM THEM' " (Gal. 3:10).

" *'He who overcomes will thus be clothed in white garments; and I will not erase his name from the book of life, and I will confess his name before My Father and before His angels'* " (Rev. 3:5).

"The beast that you saw was, and is not, and is about to come up out of the abyss and go to destruction. And those who dwell on the earth, whose name has not been written in the book of life from the foundation of the world, will wonder when they see the beast, that he was and is not and will come" (Rev. 17:8).

"And if anyone's name was not found written in the book of life, he was thrown into the lake of fire" (Rev. 20:15).

"I testify to everyone who hears the words of the prophecy of this book: if anyone adds to them, God will add to him the plagues which are written in this book" (Rev. 22:18).

"Oh that my words were written! Oh that they were inscribed in a book!" (Job 19:23).

The very Bible that you and I study each day is one of God's accounting books of the lives and testimonies of His children. All the actions of the just (saved) and unjust (unsaved) are recorded – yes, all of them. This is why it takes Jesus Christ one thousand years to get through the entire Judgment process of all past, present, and future humans. His book of deeds will be opened and all will be held in account to every deed committed – good and bad. The unsaved will be condemned for their list. The born-again children of God will be covered under the blood of the Lamb; although, Christians will still face their moment of recorded sins. The difference is that Christians are not condemned or sentenced to eternal punishment.

There are also over 3,000 references of rewards stated in the Old and New Testaments. God seems to make a big deal about recorded sins, deeds, and levels of rewards ("eternal weight of glory" - 2 Cor. 4:17). God is not promoting works or performance, but rather rewards for those who diligently walk after the Spirit according to His divine will.

God is all about testing those He loves (James 1:3). One of the most sobering tests of a man's character is his attitude and mind-set toward the use of what has been given to him to steward – like money. Men who are being considered for church or ministry leadership must pass the test of wise and godly money management (1 Tim. 3:3).

Character revealed by money management is very important. Christians are constantly warned by the Lord not even to eat a meal with a person who claims to be a so-called Christian, who is actually a manipulating swindler in money matters (1 Cor. 5:11).

One of the easiest ways I use to find out if someone is mishandling the Lord's money is requiring him to show me (his counselor) his financial records. If he gets defensive when put on the spot regarding accountability for his financial affairs, I know something is up. If that man cannot, or refuses, to produce a record of his funding and material possessions, I automatically withhold my promotion of church management. Defensiveness is usually a plea of guilt and is a mechanism to keep the confronter at bay. Therefore, all those with whom you deal who have secret greed in their hearts are most likely going to be your accusers. The love of money is literally at the root of all evil (1 Tim 6:10).

ACCOUNTING IN FAMILY LIFE

Most family men do not think in terms of an accounting system. I can tell you this; the manner in which a man handles his money is the same manner in which he handles his family. The only men that can hide one from the other are liars. This is the principle that elders are to use for determining if a man is ready for church management – look to his finances and family life. The man should not be groomed for church management until his house and bank account are in order.

The real purpose of household headship is a testing field for leadership within the kingdom of God. The moment a man manipulates his finances to satisfy self-will, he is to be put at arm's length and watched carefully.

This man is dangerous to the leadership domain of the kingdom of God. If a man is willing to trash his family for the sake of self-gain, he certainly will use the church for the same reason.

"He must be one who manages his own household well, keeping his children under control with all dignity (but if a man does not know how to manage his own household, how will he take care of the church of God?), and not a new convert, so that he will not become conceited and fall into the condemnation incurred by the devil" (1 Tim. 3:4-6).

THE SECURITY OF WOMAN

I have always said that the woman is a meter to monitor the flesh level of her husband. I listen and watch carefully to hearts and voices of women. They have been blessed with a supernatural ability to predict the downfall of their men. Their security is in the observation of watching their men handle the checkbook with integrity.

Most men think that women are secure with houses, food, clothing, spending money, and trips to the hair salon. Even though most women enjoy these things, an average Christian woman will say: "I would rather live in a cardboard box and be debt free than live a mansion with debt up to our ears." She needs to see her man monitoring the following:

- Checking accounts
- Savings
- Investments
- Legal papers (contracts, leases, birth certificates, wills, etc.)
- Licenses, permits
- Marriage certificates
- Medical records
- Insurance
- Salary and pension Information
- Real estate records
- Social Security information
- Tax records
- Vehicle titles
- So forth and so on …

Most men can't even tell you where these items are kept, let alone what the status is on each one. It is most common for men to leave those things up to "the little woman." That might be an OK plan, but the man still needs to know the status of each item and manage an adequate accounting system to monitor these securities.

Seriously, if a man cannot give immediate account to these items, how can he strategically plan for the future? God's system of provision occurs in the cycle of abasing (need) and abounding (abundance).

"I know how to get along with humble means, and I also know how to live in prosperity; in any and every circumstance I have learned the secret of being filled and going hungry, both of having abundance and suffering need" (Phil. 4:12).

It is a man's responsibility to teach his family how to adjust to these varying conditions with wise planning and preparation. He needs to put aside every penny, nickel, and dime to save for a future drought or challenge.

"On the first day of every week each one of you is to put aside and save, as he may prosper, so that no collections be made when I come" (1 Cor. 16:2).

Planning ahead is critical and absolutely necessary in God's miraculous system of accounting. In fact, he gave us ants as a natural demonstration of this life principle and command.

"Go to the ant, O sluggard, observe her ways and be wise, which, having no chief, officer or ruler, prepares her food in the summer and gathers her provision in the harvest" (Prov. 6:6-8).

CHAPTER 32

POOR MONEY MANAGERS ARE THIEVES

OK, no one really enjoys talking about this topic. The Lord is well aware of the tendencies mankind has in stealing from God, man, and self. It is simply a major ramification of the fall.

Most associate this topic with stealing money or possessions from others. Few look behind the scene of the deception of stealing. For example, the most dangerous form of stealing is not from the tithing and offerings of the Lord.

"Will a man rob God? Yet you are robbing Me! But you say, 'How have we robbed You?' In tithes and offerings" (Mal. 3:8).

Another form of stealing is not accounting for money, time, or efforts entrusted to us by an authority figure. One example would be conducting personal business on company time. How about bailing a child out of his circumstances in order to save face for you and your spouse? Is that stealing? Of course it is! There are literally thousands of ways we steal from God, man, and self. We simply refuse to take the time to look behind the walls of stealing.

Selfishness, in general, is just another fancy word for thief! In order to be selfish, one has to steal from another in order to gain for self. Too simple? Probably not. The resources and possessions of a child of God are given to us by God. He expects us to spend them on the items He purposed. As a good and righteous Father, He will hold us responsible for the blessings that He has entrusted to our care, such as money and goods. For every item or coin given to us, much more is expected of us by God. The less we have, the less is expected.

" 'From everyone who has been given much, much will be required; and to whom they entrusted much, of him they will ask all the more' " (Luke 12:48).

The Lord God is very clear on His expectations of how He wants us to handle His funding, possessions, and resources. For when we do not handle them according to the divine will of God, He considers it stealing – from Him, to be exact. Not only that, He expects this man to pay, or restitute, it all back.

"If a man gives his neighbor a donkey, an ox, a sheep, or any animal to keep for him, and it dies or is hurt or is driven away while no one is looking, an oath before the LORD shall be made by the two of them that he has not laid hands on his neighbor's property; and its owner shall accept it, and he shall not make restitution. But if it is actually stolen from him, he shall make restitution to its owner. If a man borrows anything from his neighbor, and it is injured or dies while its owner is not with it, he shall make full restitution" (Ex. 22:10-12, 14).

In reality, it is this principle of "restitution" that keeps men in debt (stealing from the rich). They do not want to face the reality of paying people back in all things. Typically, people in bondage to debt understand the concept of paying back money they have borrowed. But few understand the principle of restitution when it comes to stealing time, not returning "borrowed" possessions, and using other people for their own gain. If an indebted person really understood that unpaid debt is stealing, he might not have "borrowed" to start with.

So how many "Christian" thieves are running around the world today? More than you want to know. It is estimated that 72% of organized church attendees are in debt beyond their ability to pay their creditors back.

ACCOUNTING STOPS DEBT

Someone meticulous about accounting is rarely comfortable going into debt. Since the focus is on watching the number shrink in size, it works against itself to increase debt. Don't get me wrong, there are some who use a good accounting system to prove to themselves they can actually go into more debt. But the healthy minded person hates debt.

God oftentimes tests us in order to see just how much we can be entrusted with. Early on in his career, my wife's uncle was given an envelope containing $10,000 cash by his boss, who owned a billion dollar company.

He was instructed to hand deliver it to the bank, which he did. The boss called the bank and her uncle was given yet another mission the next day, but this time $50,000 cash was in the envelope. This went on until the amount reached $100,000 cash. With each mission, he protected the money with his heart of integrity. Over the years, as a result of this act of preservation, her uncle was advanced from "mail boy" to the vice president of the entire company. Uncle Bob's boss probably got this principle and technique from the Word of God; but still the same, it is an honorable test. God, too, uses this venue on each of us.

" 'He who is faithful in a very little thing is faithful also in much; and he who is unrighteous in a very little thing is unrighteous also in much. Therefore if you have not been faithful in the use of unrighteous wealth, who will entrust the true riches to you?' " (Luke 16:10-11).

Uncle Bob's boss needed to determine the level of danger that might have existed between his personal assistant and himself. Even though the boss obviously kept precise record of his investment, he didn't know for sure if his assistant would do the same. As a result, both were rewarded with many years of friendship, trust, and prosperity.

The same principles of accurate accounting of money are the very same principles God uses in His kingdom. There are no differences! Once a man figures that out, he then can embrace the process of accumulating wealth. The first step to increasing wealth is to account of everything he has earned, was given to him, or loaned to him.

The next step is to be a righteous manager over present and future earnings, by making debt free and wise purchases that advance the Master's way.

The final step is to carefully guard against any and all who would take away one's earnings through crafty deceptive ways, such as fruitless purchases.

A wise man will not only record all his financial and material blessings, but he also will record all the insights and ideas in which God gives him to grow as a child of God. Keeping record does not stop with saleable items, which are only the point of beginnings. Call it journaling or record keeping, it doesn't matter – just do it. Please remember: for every ounce of wisdom God puts into us, Satan will attempt to steal two. It is in this manner, he forms debt.

CHAPTER 33

LOANING TO OTHERS

Do you want to destroy a healthy relationship? Then try loaning money to a family member or friend. It would be far better to give the money with no strings attached. I have seen too many "healthy relationships" fall on the rocks over a personal loan.

Personal, corporate, or national economics built upon debt mentality are a precursor to being disciplined by God. If allowed to continue, they will without question end in bankruptcy and loss of freedom.

Freedom comes from the word picture of being freed from the bondage of debt (slavery). In order for a person, corporation, or nation to be truly free – they must be debt free. When someone takes out a loan, it places that person in the position of a slave. If this occurs within a family or friendship, trouble is soon to follow. At first, loaning money to a loved one communicates love and trust. But after a while, it musters up a much different message. If the loan is paid in full immediately, no problem. But if it is not, the relationship is about to be tested with the greatest test of all - slavery.

Generally speaking, if a loved one ever asks us to cosign on a loan, say, "No!" If he asks to borrow a few bucks, say, "No." But if we have it, give it to him anyway. If he tells us that he WILL pay it back, give it anyway - in our mind. If he pays us back – praise the Lord. If he doesn't – praise the Lord. We will have lost nothing. Many friendships and family relationships have been destroyed over a "few bucks." Even though loaning with expectation is dangerous, it is nowhere close to being as dangerous as cosigning.

TURNING A FRIEND INTO A SLAVE

Scripture clearly states that the one who borrows is the one who becomes the slave. The last I heard, no one enjoys being in bondage unless they volunteer for the job. Let's face the facts here; it is really difficult to have a dynamic relationship with someone who is enslaved to us. I certainly can work on the master's side, but the slave side becomes quite the challenge.

"The rich rules over the poor, And the borrower becomes the lender's slave" (Prov. 22:7).

On top of making our loved one a slave, we actually set them up to put us where God should be - that is NOT good. Loans indicate one of two things: the desire to have something that is not in one's budget or a desperate need due to financial pressure. It is a nonissue if the item does not fit into one's budget. If the person is experiencing financial pressure, this is typically a sign that God is about to teach this person an awesome lesson.

"Call upon Me in the day of trouble; I shall rescue you, and you will honor Me" (Psalm 50:15).

Most do not wait until God reveals the miracle in our day of trouble. We usually find some quick fix to getting out of the fix that God has fixed on us to rid ourselves of fixing fixes. Wow, what a mouthful! Lending becomes one of the human rescues, which oftentimes replaces the hand of God.

So what about those biblical passages that encourage us NOT to turn away those who want to borrow from us? The rules of engagement which God gave to His people for lending were based on helping our neighbor through a crisis. In those days, when a neighbor was in financial crisis, it affected the whole of the community. The loan was actually viewed as a gift and absolutely no interest was ever to be charged.

"You shall not charge interest to your countrymen: interest on money, food, or anything that may be loaned at interest" (Deut. 23:19).

God does not allow the charging of interest to a brother (friend) or family member, nor does He allow us to keep a person in financial bondage. This is exactly why He conducted (and still does) the release of all debt on the seventh year and the year of jubilee. This is rarely practiced anymore.

"At the end of every seven years you shall grant a remission of debts. This is the manner of remission: every creditor shall release what he has loaned to his neighbor; he shall not exact it of his neighbor and his brother, because the LORD'S remission has been proclaimed" (Deut. 15:1-2).

Even with that said, God still prefers the righteous to show mercy and give over lending.

"The wicked borrows and does not pay back, But the righteous is gracious and gives" (Psalm 37:21).

"One who is gracious to a poor man lends to the LORD, And He will repay him for his good deed" (Prov. 19:17).

As we give to those who are in need, we are actually allowing God (not that He needs our permission) to use His own resources imparted to us for His own agenda. He, God, knows where all of His storehouses are throughout the world at any given moment of every day. The children of God, who know this principle, dare not spend any of the King's money, unless the King grants permission.

" 'Give to everyone who asks of you, and whoever takes away what is yours, do not demand it back' " (Luke 6:30).

I really think that God wants us to lend, but with no expectation of any return. I know this sounds a bit odd, but the Scriptures are filled with this living life principle.

" 'But love your enemies, and do good, and lend, expecting nothing in return; and your reward will be great, and you will be sons of the Most High; for He Himself is kind to ungrateful and evil men' " (Luke 6:35).

CHAPTER 34

USING LOVED ONES FOR FINANCIAL GAIN

I am appalled at the number of "Christians" who use the term "business" for what the Bible calls usury. Through the years, I have advised more businesses, churches, and ministries than I can shake a stick at. In almost every case, I discover some hidden deception cloaked in the cloth of "business." It is important, if not critical, to understand what the Scriptures have to say about making money off of the losses of others - usury.

"If you lend money to My people, to the poor among you, you are not to act as a creditor to him; you shall not charge him interest" (Ex. 22:25).

Making money off of the pain of others is not only common nowadays, but some "children of God" have literally made a business out of it. I have even seen some that have "Christ-centered" on their literature. The ramifications of such acts of manipulation are a bit frightening.

It hinders God's blessing on the lender and borrower.

"You may charge interest to a foreigner, but to your countrymen you shall not charge interest, so that the LORD your God may bless you in all that you undertake in the land which you are about to enter to possess" (Deut. 23:20).

It downplays the fear of God.

" 'Do not take usurious interest from him, but revere your God, that your countryman may live with you. You shall not give him your silver at interest, nor your food for gain. I am the LORD your God, who brought you out of the land of Egypt to give you the land of Canaan and to be your God' " (Lev. 25:36-38).

It ultimately leads both parties away from God.

" 'In you they have taken bribes to shed blood; you have taken interest and profits, and you have injured your neighbors for gain by oppression, and you have

forgotten Me,' declares the Lord GOD. 'Behold, then, I smite My hand at your dishonest gain which you have acquired and at the bloodshed which is among you' " (Ezek. 22:12-13).

It sets up both parties to spiritually stumble.

"O LORD, who may abide in Your tent? Who may dwell on Your holy hill? (Psalm 15:1).

"He does not put out his money at interest, Nor does he take a bribe against the innocent. He who does these things will never be shaken" (Psalm 15:5).

It puts God's valuable money into the hands of the wrong people.

"He who increases his wealth by interest and usury Gathers it for him who is gracious to the poor" (Prov. 28:8).

It calls down the discipline of God on both parties.

"Then he may have a violent son who sheds blood and who does any of these things to a brother" (Ezek. 18:10).

"He lends money on interest and takes increase; will he live? He will not live! He has committed all these abominations, he will surely be put to death; his blood will be on his own head" (Ezek. 18:13).

Assuming we agree that God equates usury with extortion, then usury is an offense for which the New Testament church should experience discipline.

*"Therefore let us celebrate the feast, not with old leaven, nor with the leaven of malice and wickedness, but with the unleavened bread of sincerity and truth. I wrote you in my letter not to associate with immoral people; I did not at all mean with the immoral people of this world, or with the covetous and swindlers, or with idolaters, for then you would have to go out of the world. But actually, I wrote to you not to associate with any **so-called brother** if he is an immoral person, or covetous, or an idolater, or a reviler, or a drunkard, or a swindler--not even to eat with such a one. For what have I to do with judging outsiders? Do you not judge those who are within the church? But those who are outside, God judges.*

REMOVE THE WICKED MAN FROM AMONG YOURSELVES" (1 Cor. 5:8-13, bold mine).

I know this all sounds a bit harsh and burdensome. But the truth being said, God does not take to people using their "Christianity" to self-promote or to gain personally. These are actions the Scriptures state that God comes against in a significant way.

The Pictorial Hebrew has a striking way of saying it. Usury (interest) means "to strike with a sting of a snake, to oppress, or bite." If we look up snake or oppressor, we quickly see one of the names of Satan. If we connect the dots on this word picture, we will quickly see that charging interest is a pathway of Satan. A bit sobering don't you think?

The next time we are tempted to charge interest on a loan, consider the snake, and then consider if we are in the mood to come against the hand of God.

When a loved one comes to us for help, remember this: he is typically too embarrassed to ask for a handout. Instead, he usually asks for a loan, all the while hoping we will insist on giving it to him as a gift or a loan – without interest.

If we want him to ultimately curse us – give him a loan. If we would prefer a blessing for a lifetime, give it to him. Our gift will have many more dividends in the end.

"At this present time your abundance being a supply for their need, so that their abundance also may become a supply for your need, that there may be equality" (2 Cor. 8:14).

CHAPTER 35

SPENDING MONEY ON HOME EDUCATION

A fact I do not publicize very often is that I was given a "lifetime" status of "World Peace Ambassador" to the United Nations. It came with my service to President George W. Bush regarding the Faith-Based Initiative. Needless to say, I am a bit embarrassed by it, although there have been a few benefits to this status.

Recently, I became educated about the details and alarming growth of a "treaty" President Clinton signed with the UN (United Nations) during his presidency. This treaty poses a serious threat both to parental rights and US sovereignty, as well as, to public and private education. The UNCRC (United Nations Convention on the Rights of the Child) dictates not only that the federal government must intrude into the family sphere to an unprecedented degree, but also how the federal government is to monitor and govern the actions of our families through the US Department of Education (phase one implemented in 2010). Parental rights would be replaced by "the best interests of the child" as defined, ultimately, by an 18 member international committee appointed by the UN, in Switzerland.

One of the grave misunderstandings of George W. Bush was his "No Child Left Behind" project, which by the way, was for the strict purpose of derailing Clinton's approval of the UNCRC. This is why his wife, current Secretary of State Hillary Rodham Clinton, wrote the book *It Takes a Village: And Other Lessons Children Teach Us*. The unofficial plan is that when she becomes President, her administration will incorporate the UNCRC as the US standard of reporting child rights and will move forward with the new UN Child Curriculum. Since her husband's signature, the UNCRC plan has been adopted by every nation in the world except for two - the United States is one of them, thanks to President Bush. Question: If President Clinton signed the "treaty," why is the US one of the two who has not adopted the full plan? Answer: It must be ratified (given formal approval). This is why there is still time.

Nations, which have ratified the UNCRC, must make an initial report to the Committee on the Rights of the Child within two years of ratification. They must then report to and appear before the Committee every five years to measure their progress on implementation of the Convention. This is why public schools are being pressured to place "documentation above education." All this is prep work in order for the US to ratify the UNCRC. The Committee responds to the country reports with observations and suggestions for continued implementation of the UNCRC.

What the UN is not telling the nations is that they have a school curriculum coming that will replace all National Standardized Government School Education. This curriculum is designed to place every child in the entire world on one single educational learning track.

It is so easy to blow this off as "blah, blah, blah." But the truth being said, it will affect every American citizen whether they care about family life or not. This plan will affect every public and private school, homeschools, every parent, grandparent, child care worker, and any human who has contact with children. In many countries today, thousands of school teachers and parents have been arrested for upsetting children or "coming against the rights of a child." This is a serious crisis our country is facing. (Learn more at http://www.parentalrights.org)

So really - what is the purpose of the home? The home has always been the foundation of a learning center, place of warm hospitality, center of creativity, a nursing center, and ministry headquarters. When the world, the flesh, and the devil attack this command center, all "hell" breaks loose on the heart of the church.

LEARNING CENTER

Most think of "homeschoolers" when the home is referenced as a "learning center." The truth of the matter is the concept of "homeschooling" is no older than the American hippy. On the other hand, the home being viewed as a center for learning has been around since Adam and Eve.

If and when the family functions as the Holy Scriptures are laid out, the basic ingredients of learning are already present. Some of these qualities are acceptance, security, modeling, discipline, organization, consistency, and the structure of the church.

When learning in and from the home is related to living everyday life and is carefully motivated by planned and unplanned activities, we have the makings of a real to life school. The home as a learning center is to be viewed as teaching our children every moment of each day – not just when the public school bell rings.

"You shall teach them diligently to your sons and shall talk of them when you sit in your house and when you walk by the way and when you lie down and when you rise up" (Deut. 6:7).

When parents "farm out" their teaching responsibilities to strangers, they are sure to get strange teachings. Plus, this not only is a confession of ignorance, they lose their prerogative to communicate with their children, love on them, and grow them up into the ways they so desire. I cannot think of anyone who knows the needs of a child better than the parents of that child. Since over 50% of our children grow up in a one parent home, this privilege is fading more and more into the sunset of the yesteryears. Therefore, I will speak to those parents who are interested in capturing every moment they can with their children.

SPEND MONEY ON BUILDING CHARACTER

God has blessed children with His gifting before they are born. It is the parents' responsibility to lead the child to Christ in order for the Holy Spirit to awaken these gifts to be used for God. He has also blessed children with a type of faith that is simple, pure, and a model for even those who have been selected to go to heaven.

" 'Truly I say to you, unless you are converted and become like children, you will not enter the kingdom of heaven' " (Matt. 18:3).

Through these gifts, the parent is to assist the child in extracting the character qualities of Christ. They also help the child practice these qualities until Christ is empowered in them to do it through them.

Each child needs to learn to stand in his faith as an individual by the ripe age of thirteen. Yes, I said thirteen. Hebrew manners and laws require of the parents to have their child ready for adult transfer between ten and thirteen. That does not mean the child leaves the home. It just means the parent has trained the child in the basics of life. Statistics show us today that the average age of departure from the parent is between 25 and 30 years of age. There certainly seems to be something wrong with that picture.

Children need the ability to stand in their faith, alone if need be, at an early age. This way the child can stand up to the attacks of the enemy when the parents are not around to protect him. If should be every parent's desire to have their children born-again at an early age and to be equipped to allow Christ to live in and through them. This is difficult to accomplish if the child is being educated outside of the home – possible, but very difficult.

CHAPTER 36

FINANCING FUN AND FELLOWSHIP

Did you grow up in one of those homes where it was "grand central station" for all your friends? I hope so. The absolute best financial investment a man can make is turning his home into a fun and educational place for the whole neighborhood. Bringing disruption to your own home is better than sending your children out into a problematic world where you cannot supervise them. Plus, God promises to bless the family who shows hospitality.

"Is this not the fast which I choose, to loosen the bonds of wickedness, to undo the bands of the yoke, And to let the oppressed go free and break every yoke? Is it not to divide your bread with the hungry and bring the homeless poor into the house; when you see the naked, to cover him; And not to hide yourself from your own flesh? Then your light will break out like the dawn, and your recovery will speedily spring forth; and your righteousness will go before you; the glory of the LORD will be your rear guard" (Isa. 58:6-8).

Many Christians don't realize this, but hospitality is a huge deal to God. So much so, that He literally mandated it as one of the primary requirements of being a godly woman.

"...having a reputation for good works; and if she has brought up children, if she has shown hospitality to strangers, if she has washed the saints' feet, if she has assisted those in distress, and if she has devoted herself to every good work" (1 Tim. 5:10).

Our Husband, Jesus, has offered us very specific instructions regarding the motives we should adopt when it comes to hospitality. We are not to be hospitable for any other reason but to qualify our service to Christ.

"And He also went on to say to the one who had invited Him, 'When you give a luncheon or a dinner, do not invite your friends or your brothers or your relatives or rich neighbors, otherwise they may also invite you in return and that will be

your repayment. But when you give a reception, invite the poor, the crippled, the lame, the blind, and you will be blessed, since they do not have the means to repay you; for you will be repaid at the resurrection of the righteous' " (Luke 14:12-14).

That certainly sheds a completely different light on hospitality. Most, including me, consider hospitality to be opening your home to family and friends. The word hospitality in the Hebrew means "place of healing." We get our English word "hospital" from this word picture.

There are four primary blessings that come with hospitality:

God's attributes are revealed, not concealed. People in our homes see our families functioning not only in word, but also in deed. The best way to reach a hurting person is by action. When these poor, crippled, lame, and blind experience our families working together to accomplish the Great Commission, healing will follow.

It opens up a school of learning for our guest. This is where the rubber meets the road when it comes to home education. Our guest will watch or in the case of the blind, listen, to how Christianity really works. For my family, it has given us many opportunities of ministering to others by simply answering their questions.

In sharing, our guests are invited into life change. A family should look at their home as a tool to help and encourage others through drink, food, fellowship, and many times, the shirt off of one's back.

The home is purified in Christ. People in our homes notice little things like: what we have on our walls, music we have playing in the background, books on our shelves, or seeing how disciplined our children are. When they walk into our houses, they should almost taste the Living Water of Jesus Christ.

THE HOME IS THE CENTER OF CREATIVITY

Some of the most successful businesses in the world started in the home and oftentimes by families who home educated their children. This means income for the home keeps mom from the external workplace and helps dad keep his heart turned toward home. Men classically have their faces turned in the direction of money and this is one significant way to help dad keep his focus on the family.

Did you know it would be next to impossible for the "Proverbs 31 woman" to do what she did if she had to maintain an external job in the marketplace? It is true; a significant amount of time, dedication, and resources are needed for her to accomplish this feat. This is no ice cream dipping woman being described here. She is diligent in all aspects of life. I am married to one of these ladies. They are hardworking servants of the Lord!

People are rarely creative unless they are given the time, resources, and encouragement to be creative.

THE HOME IS A NURSING CENTER

Most "Proverbs 31" women know this is a duh. A home filled with safety and peace adds healing to each of the family members. The home should be a refuge that family, friends, and strangers can come and be nourished.

Moms in particular are the "doctors" of the home. They are quick to know how to bandage the emotional, relational, and physical boo-boos. As I have watched my wife through the years, I have seen seven primary tools in her "doctor's bag."

Heart-Healthy Attitude: She maintains a home filled with accountability for attitudes of forgiveness and healing between each of her members. She has an uncanny ability to clear the conscience on a day-to-day basis.

Heart-Healthy Foods: As we see in Proverbs 31, this woman has the special ability to plan and prepare meals that are heart-healthy and comforting to the family. Yes, I said comfort foods. There is NOTHING wrong with comfort foods. The tastes, smells, and textures of foods create positive memories that will bring that family together for years to come!

Heart-Healthy Fasting: Believe it or not, God created our bodies to fast (withhold from foods) on a regular basis. Moms should work with the heads of the home to set aside one meal a week to fast and pray together as a family. No, the family does not go off in different directions, but rather sits around the dinner table and prays!

Heart-Healthy Dental Care: Did you brush your teeth, son? Moms seem to have this special knack to remember to make sure their family is brushing their teeth. She knows that a healthy mouth is a healthy checkbook and dad usually likes that.

Heart-Healthy Safety: Don't get me started on this one. I have watched my wife watch over her family like a barn swallow watching her nest my entire marriage. She is a mama bear out to save her cubs AND her papa bear. With most women, if someone messes with their family, he is going to hear about it.

Heart-Healthy Cleaning: I cannot tell you how many times I have gone to put on my shoes and they are gone. For most women, a clean home is a sign of a clean heart. This certainly is the case for our home. We all help mama pick up and put the entire house in order each night before our heads hit the pillows.

Heart-Healthy Prayers: I know God has given women a special desire to pray. They remind their children and encourage their husbands to pray, pray, and pray a little bit more. We have literally seen miracles in our home through the years because of my wife's passion to lift her husband up to prayer. How does she do this? Simple: she asks me. If I say no, well, whose fool would I be? Women can train their men to pray by simply asking them to do it.

When people ask me what is in my wallet, I say, "My family." I am a firm believer that if the family goes, the church suffers. If the church suffers, the community becomes dysfunctional. After a dysfunctional community comes the collapse of the whole nation, and ultimately, the world.

CHAPTER 37

FINANCING HOMESPUN MINISTRY

Did you know that the home is the heart of a nation? It is true. The Hebrew structure of family reveals that the head of a home is called a governor and community authority is to rest upon his left shoulder. The view comes from our observations of Jesus Christ. In the first family, God is the Father/Patriarch of the family, Jesus is the husband, and the Church is the Bride. From this first family, God has established cities, nations, and even the world.

The early Church grew in numbers and effectiveness primarily due to the home being viewed as the primary base of the local church. I know – you were taught that the family is an extension of the local church down on the corner of Jefferson and Franklin, but it simply is NOT true. Early indwelt Christians would meet daily in various homes to exhort each other from the Word of God, pray, and then be released to the world to accomplish the Great Commission.

Today, home churches are the wave of the future, but are still considered the "odd man out." I can assure you that in due time, the home church structure WILL return and be the norm for all true indwelt Christians. It's funny though; most local churches in the world are underground churches that meet in homes, shacks, and caves. But here in America, if a church doesn't have a building – it's not a REAL church. Personally, I think America is in for a serious reality check. After spending the past 10 years studying the history of countries from all over the world, my conclusion is that America is the most deceived and arrogant of them all. Well, enough of my soap box – let's get back to how we should be spending our money.

In spite of the American view of "home-based ministries," homes abound with opportunities for effective spiritual outreach. Each of these outreach opportunities is and will continue to be used by Jesus Christ to accomplish

His mission. These outreach venues also provide a perfect direction for funds spent by the family income. Here are a few ways to consider:

HOME-BASED BIBLE STUDIES: A good example of this is my dear wife. She has been sponsoring women's Bible Studies in and out of our home for many years. I rarely question the moneys spent on DVD's or workbooks to accomplish such a mission. Many family and friends are introduced to the truest things about Christ through this venue. Most community-based local churches today do not teach the core victorious truths of "Not I but Christ." Due to this problem, my wife and I are very quick to provide such teachings for the community at large. It needs to be noted that we do not advocate separating singles or teenagers from these groups. Men's groups should be 13 years of age on up and the same for women's groups. Segregation of the Body of Christ IS what destroyed the local church – thanks to Thomas Jefferson.

HOME FELLOWSHIPS: Home churches are not as scary as one might think. If the local community-based church used "home fellowships" as a part of its growth plan, most wouldn't think twice about attending one. But, to actually start a Home Fellowship that functions like the local church – well, that is a different matter altogether. We really are a funny kind of people. God is not into 501c3 government run and approved certifications. He is into building up the Body of Christ for the work of service unto the accomplishment of the Great Commission. Home Fellowships are a perfect breeding ground for life upon life discipleship.

MISSION PROJECTS: Our family has supported mission projects and missionaries all over the world for most of our adult lives. We have stories of touched lives because of it. One time, my eldest daughter and I made a mission trek over to Kenya, travelled over 4 hours in a jeep until the jeep could not drive any further, and then walked another mile or two – just to reach our sponsored child and her family. It was one of our life adventures that we will remember for eternity. Mission moneys should not only go "overseas," but also in your backyard. Spend some hard earned cash on turning your home into a mission project, like packing food boxes that go to local needy people.

Mission service projects build family, fellowship, and community. Not only that, but they teach others how to serve and give THEIR hard earned moneys to others.

NEIGHBORHOOD BUILDING: One idea that occasionally works, depending on your neighbors, is neighborhood street parties, God-style. Once a year (or more), turn your front lawn and driveway into a party center. Put up a tent, heat up the grill, and provide plenty of family friendly activities – all directed at getting to know one another. You don't have to turn it into an evangelism drive, just have some fun. Fun, food, and fellowship oftentimes speak more to your neighbors than your preaching; although, always be ready for a good preach.

VISITING WIDOWS AND ORPHANS: The growing reality of our world around us is that more and more families are becoming fatherless and oftentimes without parents. Yes, I said parents. This results in grandparents raising their children's children, which is becoming a problem of epidemic proportions. Independence, divorce, and striving for the "almighty buck" are turning grandpa and grandma's place into orphanages. This makes quality outreach for indwelt Christian families even more necessary than ever before. Plus, God actually requires it of all of His children.

"Pure and undefiled religion in the sight of our God and Father is this: to visit orphans and widows in their distress, and to keep oneself unstained by the world" (James 1:27).

TAKING CARE OF MOM AND POPS: I think you would agree with me that we live in a "throw away" society! This horrific trend is becoming such a problem, that the UN has started a campaign called "euthanasia." Euthanasia is the process of expelling (killing off) the elderly, handicapped, and terminally weak. The government has already proven that "nursing homes" and nursing care are so overpriced that something has to be done. Well, the fix to "being done" is euthanasia. I hate to admit it, but I don't think we as a people will be able to turn this one around. The generation of youth today is NOT going to stop and reformat their lives to include having their elderly parents grow old within their emergent households. It just is not going to happen. You might find a few families clinging to these old school values; but overall, euthanasia is the only solution to this depraved world.

In saying that, the wonderful opportunities available to help these elderly people in the community becomes massive. For indwelt Christian families to serve in this way is a perfect way to show their own grandchildren how to care for their own grandparents. We must attack the global issues with local steps and this is a great way to start. By helping the elderly, family members are put in the position to rethink the ways of the world. This can be accomplished by going to the local retirement center. Or better yet, find several elderly people in town that can't afford professional care. This is where the real need is. Pour your money there and you will gain the attention of God.

HIGHER STANDARD OF LIVING: Believe it or not, the most reliable way of using your home for quality outreach is to observe the habits of your home. Some of the items to consider are:

- Set a time to put the cell phones on the shelf each night.
- Set a schedule for TV viewing. On non-viewing days/nights, plan creative relationship building activities.
- Make a decision not to answer phones during meal preparation or dinner times.
- Develop a habit to have mealtime devotions – Oswald Chambers is our favorite.
- Plan your "dining out" times and spend more time doing family cooking.
- Pay less on hiring others to do household chores and do them as a family.
- Agree to stop spending money on "junk food."
- Take family walks – invite neighbors to go with you.
- Take time to read – even if it is just for fun.
- Develop new habits of getting up earlier and starting your day right.

There are so many things we can do to save money in and around the home, just by not being so lazy. Laziness is very expensive. The ways of a lazy person are destructive. My children, and now grandchildren, hear me speak often about the ways of the ant. These little creatures are some of the hardest working examples of all of God's creation.

"Go to the ant, O sluggard, Observe her ways and be wise, which, having no chief, Officer or ruler, Prepares her food in the summer And gathers her provision in the harvest. How long will you lie down, O sluggard? When will you arise from your sleep? A little sleep, a little slumber, a little folding of the hands to rest--Your poverty will come in like a vagabond and your need like an armed man. A worthless person, a wicked man, Is the one who walks with a perverse mouth, Who winks with his eyes, who signals with his feet, Who points with his fingers" (Prov. 6:6-13).

CHAPTER 38

THE PRICE OF A WORKING MOTHER

Recently, I was reading some up-to-date research on the price our nation has had to pay for the mothers of our children working outside the home. The results were alarming, to say the least. The reason why Hillary Clinton said that she wrote the book "It Takes a Village: And Other Lessons Children Teach Us" is because there are few mothers at home to raise a child. This is quite a confession from a working mother.

I wish I could say that the reason mothers want to work outside of the home is because they are forced to, by our present state of a fatherless society. But the truth being said, this is not the number one surveyed reason. The primary reason stated was that the men won't work outside of the home. I must admit, this is one of those times I will have to agree with a worldly statistic. It is proven there are more men in the unemployment line than women. It is also a fact that men tend to be lazier, dishonest in the work place, and default to women to take care of them like nursing mothers. It was also stated that men tend to work for the weekends, to take a vacation, or to simply purchase that next toy. Women, on the other hand, tend to work to pay the bills. The result of our men not growing up and putting their toys in the closet has turned our society into a feminized dominant workplace.

The ramifications of a mother working outside the home are significant. I would like to share with you the top 10 ramifications that I have seen.

ONE - SHE LIVES IN VIOLATION TO SCRIPTURE: Certainly one of the most popular and less quoted verses on the topic is Titus 2:4-5: "so that they may encourage the young women to love their husbands, to love their children, to be sensible, pure, workers at home, kind, being subject to their own husbands, so that the word of God will not be dishonored."

The Lord designed women to be workers of the home and this is no small task. Since the home is the center of the nation, not having a mother there to tend to it throws the whole of the nation off balance. Timothy, Paul's spiritual son, said this about even widowed mothers: "Therefore, I want younger widows to get married, bear children, keep house, and give the enemy no occasion for reproach" (1 Tim. 5:14). The portion of the Scripture that screams out a warning to me is "give the enemy no occasion for reproach." If we were to give the enemy a reproach in this matter, he would have to get the women outside of the home. He, if anyone, knows that in order to drop the nation, you must send the mother bear away from her cubs. If the mother bear is away, the government is sure to play – the role of the mother that is. God has warned us many times that when a woman is not in the home, she become boisterous and full of rebellion.

"She is boisterous and rebellious, her feet do not remain at home" (Prov. 7:11).

TWO - HER CHILDREN RUN WILD: Let's face it: no one can take the place of a mother – not even a village. This adage of her going to work, making the bacon, and frying it up in the pan is a sarcastic spoof on God's mandates, not to mention an insult to men. Children not only need their mother, they want her – 24/7. God has placed it within all children to run to their mothers for comfort, nurturing, and application of spiritual growth. When she is not there, the child is forced to be his own god. That is exactly what has happened. We have a world full of self-centered cotton-topped godheads running wild like beasts.

THREE - SHE ONLY ACTS FULFILLED: Faking it until you make it is one of the truest statements for working mothers. They might act like they have it all together and don't mind NOT being with their nursing babes – but the fact is, they are torn up inside. If they aren't, they are more like the enemy than they realize. God designed all of us to discover the trinity of our personal identities - spiritual, relational, and physical. The only true and fair way a woman can discover her full identity in Christ is to discover and walk in the purpose for which she was put on this earth.

Scripture clearly marks the pathway for woman to be the "helpmate" to her husband and if not married, to her father (Gen. 2:18). Now there is a popular passage, not! When women try to act like men and men try to act like women, the children turn gay. Why is the gay society the fastest growing movement in the world today? It is due to the fact that men and women have completely swapped roles. Because of this, God is about to turn the world on its ears.

FOUR - SHE MAKES A TRAIN WRECK OUT OF HER MARRIAGE: Men are feeble without their women. We are not designed to be alone; in fact, we can't function without a wife or mother unless God grants us special skills to do so. I personally believe the reason why most men go outside the home to gain female affection is because he cannot find it at home. I understand this is not a catchall, but it certainly is one of the main contributors to this moral dilemma.

The love of God between a husband and wife is perfected when they realize just how much they not only need each other, but need each to function in their God-given role. When marriage partners act or function like they don't need each other, they are covertly communicating to God that they do not need Him. When the woman of the house thinks she does not need her husband or children, sooner or later, she transfers her loyalty and love to those outside the home.

FIVE - TRANSFERRING AFFECTIONS TO OTHERS: Did you know that when a woman works for a man, husband or not, she demonstrates emotions of affection, loyalty, and service? It could be stated that she naturally functions as a wife or daughter to the man. When she is at work, it is her responsibility to please her employer and fulfill the desires of his heart – work that is. She is to honor, submit, and quickly respond to her authorities. Needless to say, the bulk of women in the workplace are not like this when they come home to their husbands. The reason stated is, "They pay me to honor, submit, and obey – you don't." Well, that confession proves its own point. It's all about the "almighty buck."

Did you know that over 90% of the adulteress affairs that take place are introduced in the marketplace? This might be the reason. Women are designed to work for their husbands and fathers. The same rule goes for men; ideally, they should not hire women as their assistants unless they are blood or adoptive family members. Women are naturally going to compare woman to woman and man to another man. If her boss is "nicer" than her husband, particularly to her, then affection issues will multiply.

In 1870, thirteen percent of the women of America worked outside of the home. Almost without exception, these were single women working in one of two fields, secretarial or nursing. By 1970, forty percent of the women of America worked outside their homes. By 1991, it was sixty-nine percent, and in 1994, it was about seventy-one percent. They are no longer only single women, but also married women and mothers who have children and teenagers at home. In 2008, over eighty-nine percent of all women worked outside of the home.

If you are like most, you are sick to death of hearing these statistics; in fact, statistics show that you have become immune to them. You and I rarely take the time to respond to statistics like: America holds the highest divorce rate of any free country in the world; American women abort/kill 1.5 million babies a year; only thirteen percent of our children now grow up in a family of one husband, one wife and one set of children; not to mention, the level of teen pregnancies. Crime, murder, suicide, and all types of abuses are on the rise in our "Christian nation under God." It does not take more than a junior high kid to conclude that there is something very wrong with our society.

Sin is like water from a broken dam – it will always flow downhill and is certain to fill every crack and crevice it comes in contact with. The blame can be placed in many directions, but there is one ravine that is sure to absorb its flow – working mothers. The sin of devaluing motherhood in America is what I consider one of the greatest sins known to all generations. We live in such a godless society that women put their motherhood on hold to lead ministries or even become President of the United States, all the while their children are running to other "mothers" to find comfort and guidance. Who are these "other mothers?" Public or private school teachers of course. When a mother is caught between two worlds, she typically is left without one in the end.

SIX - CAUGHT BETWEEN TWO WORLDS: The work world is exactly that – a world in and of itself. It is a simple truth that the field we apply our hands to becomes the home that we will serve. If a wife or mother does not find contentment in her role as a mother or wife, she is certain to find herself with one foot in two worlds – the marketplace and the home. Each make demands and the one that pays the best will win out on who she answers.

Jesus said, "No one can serve two masters; for either he will hate the one and love the other, or he will be devoted to one and despise the other. You cannot serve God and wealth" (Matt. 6:24).

Since we just learned that no one can serve two masters, this mother will sooner or later decide which world will become her primary master and means of love, acceptance, and approval.

SEVEN - SHE WILL CRACK UNDER PRESSURE: Women are made by God to be the emotive aspect to all relationships, particularly in those she shares with her husband and children. When a working mother works outside the home, she sets herself up for increased pressure spiritually, psychologically, and physically. These three elements will produce a great deal of stress. What she does with this stress is up to her. BUT most, eighty-three percent, divorce their first and primary master – their husbands. As for their children, well – that is why we have daycare.

EIGHT - SHE BECOMES IRRESPONSIBLE: This issue is no different than time management in all arenas of life. Whatever we give our time, energy, and skill to will obviously consume that portion of investment. Whatever the remainder of the whole is left, well – that is what is left. We can't make more time. We can drink more coffee for more energy, but we cannot make more time. When each of us needs more time, there is only one place to get it – steal it from another priority. If a mother gives her resources to a job outside of the home, in due time, she will suffer the cost of less time with God, husband, and then children. Any woman, man, or child who steals time designated by God for another is a thief!

NINE - SHE BECOMES A BAD ROLE MODEL: When you meet a mother who is functioning "effectively" in two worlds, just know that she has worked her tail to the bone mastering the art of suppressing her pain. These mothers may appear to be doing OK, but the truth being said, they are exemplifying a bad and corrupt role model for their children. Supermoms are usually superficial moms, because they simply do not have the time to apply much more effort than that of the superficial.

TEN - SHE IS TYPICALLY A SPENDER: I'm not sure why, but most working mothers are "shopaholics." The only thing that I can stamp to this is that they somehow believe they deserve a reward for being such hard workers and having to sacrifice so much to do what they do. Needless to say, between this issue and paying for daycare, fuel, food, etc., the "second paycheck" is usually shot. Careful evaluation of the deception of the "second paycheck" reveals that it is an unprofitable investment. In fact, many women describe it as "throwing money to the wind." The women that make it work are rare, but the average house scenario is that it drives them deeper into debt.

I know that my style of writing is bit "tongue and cheek," but my heart is to assist and restore the family values of God back into biblical family. I understand that many mothers are forcibly put into situations where they "have to work," but that does not mean that we should not teach our children, grandchildren, or others the pure truth of God's best versus mankind's seconds.

It is my hope that you openly rejoice in the fullness of God's Truth without exchanging it for a lower level of understanding that has found its way into our churches as primary doctrines. Stand with me, my family, and many others in touting the purest form of Truth – that of, "Not I but Christ in me."

CHAPTER 39

CONNECTION OF MONEY & A GOOD NAME

"A good name is to be more desired than great wealth, Favor is better than silver and gold" (Prov. 22:1).

The Word of God talks about four primary reasons why it is so important to have a "good name." Also, God states six basic requirements in order to obtain that "good name."

I grew up in a home where a good name was NOT a priority, nor was it important! We did not practice a lifestyle that represented God and we did not honor our parents, nor have a proper mind-set toward business. It appeared that my parents really didn't care what got passed down to their children. The result was all six of their children developed a lifestyle of living from hand to mouth. The most grievous consequence of growing up in a home that could care less about having a good name was that our name was no good - it carried little value in the community we lived in. The only way to break free from this generational sin is to begin living off the reputation of another and this is exactly what I did. After struggling for many years of attempting to live off the name of another (name dropping), I found the right name to hide behind – that of Jesus Christ. Since that day, I have found success not only in reputation, but in being successful in my sphere of influence.

Let's take a look at the Word and review the four primary reasons why it is critical for us to have a good name:

ONE - INDWELT CHRISTIANS REPRESENT GOD'S NAME. The fact is, we indwelt Christians are the only Bible that the majority of the world will ever see. When we make it known that we are born-again Christians, we invite others of disbelief to test the name we represent. This is accomplished through the way we handle insults, persecutions, and distress. They will watch closely every business and personal transaction we make, in order to see if it actually represents, or matches, how God Himself would transact. The Word tells us that we are "known and read of all men." We are oftentimes the only Bible that most humans will ever read.

"You are our letter, written in our hearts, known and read by all men" (2 Cor. 3:2).

TWO - HONORING OUR PARENTS WITH GOD'S NAME: A fact that indwelt Christians cannot ignore is that the first commandment, with a promise from God, is "honor your father and mother" (Ex 20:12). Success spiritually, psychologically, and financially is directly related to honoring our parents. The promise from God in this passage is that if we do, things will go well with us. In other words, we will be successful in all that we do (Eph. 6:1-3). If we do not honor our parents, Proverbs 28:7 tells us that we will be gluttonous and a shame to our fathers. If I remember correctly, gluttons are not some of God's favored people.

THREE: WHAT WE REPRESENT IS PASSED ON TO OUR CHILDREN. If we take the above passage literally, it is far more important to pass on to our children a "good name" over a financial inheritance. In many cases, much like myself, this is the only legacy that we CAN pass on to our children that has intrinsic value. Once we get to the ripe age of 50, we begin to realize that most of our lives were either fighting against our parents' reputations or gaining the blessings that came with their "good name." Proverbs 10:7 tells us, "The memory of the righteous is blessed, but the name of the wicked will rot." The rotting process I am referring to is the warring we do in fighting off the consequences of the bad or corrupt reputation of our parents.

FOUR: PARENTAL REPUTATIONS PRODUCING RIGHTEOUSNESS AND SUCCESS. Anyone who is remotely successful knows that a good name and solid reputation is the beginning, or gateway, to being successful. One of the first things I immediately look for, in discipling individuals troubled with being able to succeed, are issues of parents with "bad reputations." This issue is not always true, but most of the time it is and it helps me show the individual what the Word has to say about the topic. This is so they don't pass it on to their children. However, the answer is always the same: identity in Christ.

The lesson here is quite obvious – those who do not hide behind the name and reputation of God are robbed of all forms of success. Not only that, but these people usually live under a constant strain of being in debt, not only financially, but in all areas of life. Exchanging one's identity from self to Christ is the only way to be free from this predictable bondage.

There are a few requirements for embracing the identity of Christ and His glorious name. The Exchanged Life, "Not I but Christ," plays a major part in an indwelt Christian's life when it comes to embracing the freedom from having a "bad name."

The first thing we need to realize is that there is no power in the name(s) of man – not one ounce! It doesn't matter how much money, fame, or influence the man obtains. In fact, the more he tries, the less God gives him. God has a principle of life in place that actually promotes the opposite effect. Jesus said, "But many who are first will be last; and the last, first" (Matt. 19:30). It needs to be noted that for those people who strive for a "good name" outside of Christ, God works to put that person in last place. Power and name have such dependence on each other that the Scriptures rarely separate them. In Acts 4:7 it says, "When they had placed them in the center, they began to inquire, 'By what power, or in what name, have you done this?' " From eternity past, God has known that all things are done through power and a name. This is why it is so important we understand this principle. It is for this very purpose that people are raised up – in order to demonstrate power, resulting in a name being proclaimed throughout the world (Rom. 9:17). Now the question comes into play, "By who's name do we gain power?" Since there are only two resources of power, Jesus Christ and Satan, that leaves us with a sobering decision.

"In the name of our Lord Jesus, when you are assembled, and I with you in spirit, with the power of our Lord Jesus" (1 Cor. 5:4).

Paul makes a couple mind-bending proclamations. First, he points out that "in the name" is the source of their gathering. Secondly, he is laying the foundation for his ability to accomplish an act that requires power to sustain and thus, proclaims that what he is about to do is done in the name and power of Jesus Christ. What was he about to do?

"I have decided to deliver such a one to Satan for the destruction of his flesh, so that his spirit may be saved in the day of the Lord Jesus" (1 Cor. 5:5).

He demonstrates an act that through the ages has become the least preached Scripture in all of Christendom. He uses the name of Jesus Christ to turn a resistant person, who defies the counsel of God through church leaders, over to Satan – the second and only name and power known to the spiritual world. The obvious reason he does this is to stop this young man's ability to be successful in his sin. Even more thought provoking, he does this for the sole purpose of providing Salvation for him. The underlying principle here is that God uses the name and power of Satan to return people back to the name and power of God. On a more practical level, God uses the deception of self (man believing that his name and power has meaning and purpose) to lead them back to His name and power.

As a discipler/counselor of 30+ years, I have found that most self-proclaimed "Christians" believe there are three powers in the world – God, Satan, and man. The truth being said, there are only two, God and Satan. What that leaves us with is that the more Satan deceives people into thinking they can be their own power, the more secondhand followers he will obtain. In God's reality, those who practice "self" are actually submitting to the power and name of Satan. Too harsh of a reality for you? Well, the only words that come to mind are: Get over it. Truth is truth and we as humans have no power in our own efforts or name.

Since the entire world is driven by money, fame, and influence, we can now see how the enemy (Satan) has a perfect, from his perspective, environment established for his soon and short-lived world leadership. Far above all who think of themselves to be self-ruled, having authority, or dominion, God will put each and every one of them under His feet. After He does that, He will grant His own Son to be the name of all names and power of all powers – for the remainder of eternity (Eph. 1:21-23).

So there you have it! This is the reason that a "good name" is worth more than all the finances in the entire world. In the end, it won't matter how much we have, but it will matter how much of Him we have. Those who know the Scriptures know that the process of knowing and having all of God is through Salvation – which is the process of becoming a Bridal member of Jesus Christ. Our marriage union with Christ grants us the privilege of coming under His name, which gives us access to His inheritance and power from eternity past, present, and future, forever and ever.

CHAPTER 40

REQUIREMENTS OF A GOOD NAME

"A Psalm of David. O LORD, who may abide in Your tent? Who may dwell on Your holy hill? He who walks with integrity, and works righteousness, And speaks truth in his heart. He does not slander with his tongue, Nor does evil to his neighbor, Nor takes up a reproach against his friend; In whose eyes a reprobate is despised, But who honors those who fear the LORD; He swears to his own hurt and does not change; He does not put out his money at interest, Nor does he take a bribe against the innocent. He who does these things will never be shaken" (Psalm 15:1-5).

Having a good name is worth more than any and all accomplishments a man could ever obtain. In the above passage, David tells us that only those who walk in integrity, do works that are righteous, speak the truth, refuse to speak ill of others, and take up the reproach of their friends are worthy enough to dwell in the tent of the living God. Well, there are six basic requirements that need to be fulfilled before this can happen.

Being a people who are true to their word. Being true to our word is rare and in fact, impossible, without Christ doing it through us. God gives ongoing warnings to those of us who resist Christ's mind (inside of us) in being True to His own Word (also inside of us). Yes, the Word of God lives and dwells within our mortal soul if we are born-again. Christ is the only One who can actually be True to the Father's Word, by faithfully fulfilling our commitments through us. Let's examine a few of the areas of "keeping our word."

- Marriage vows
- Commitment to serving God
- Reading the Word
- Paying our tithes and offerings
- Commitments made to others
- Being on time

- Being a person of integrity

Returning what we have borrowed from others. One of the most common ways to damage our reputation (name) is by not returning money, possessions, or "promises" to others. In fact, it is stealing – that is if you go by the Hebrew definition. The Word even goes as far as calling us "wicked" if we don't (Psalm 37:21). Most people borrow without making any record of what and when they borrowed. This is usually because when we borrow, we are suffering with such urgency to obtain relief from what we are missing, that we borrow out of desperation. Bad habit. If there is anything we have borrowed and have not yet returned, we are stealing. It doesn't matter how much time has passed, or from whom we have borrowed it – by not returning it, we are breaking Christ's mandate (Word) within us. Let's examine the short list:

- Money
- Books
- Tools
- Food
- Pen or pencil
- Clothes
- And the list goes on from here

Justly weighing all decisions and transactions. One of the passages that remains uncomfortable for me is Proverbs 16:11, "A just weight and scales belong to the LORD; all the weights of the bag are His concern." This means that God's watches us in every decision made – seeking to discover if we will be honest in all of our transactions. Any form of dishonesty in one of our decisions is not only stealing, it is sin. Since we have no power to be just and balanced, we must rely upon Christ in us to do so. If we tip the scale even but an ounce, God considers it an abomination (Prov. 11:1). The Word refers to it as a false weight or measure, which is called stealing.

"Can I justify wicked scales and a bag of deceptive weights? For the rich men of the city are full of violence, her residents speak lies, and their tongue is deceitful in their mouth. So also I will make you sick, striking you down, Desolating you

because of your sins. You will eat, but you will not be satisfied, and your vileness will be in your midst. You will try to remove for safekeeping, But you will not preserve anything, and what you do preserve I will give to the sword. You will sow but you will not reap. You will tread the olive but will not anoint yourself with oil; and the grapes, but you will not drink wine" (Mic. 6:11-15).

In order to avoid being desolated because of this sin, we need to carefully examine the ways we may be yielding to our flesh to gain versus allowing Christ in us to breed contentment.

- Being late for appointments
- Choosing the largest portion of that which we are sharing
- Stealing from our employment (time, pencils, etc.)
- Not fulfilling our job description at work
- Taking things without asking – assuming
- Failing to claim defects we caused and returning the item for a new one
- Exaggerating
- Negotiating a deal that puts the seller in loss of profit
- Taking sick days when we're not sick
- Etc.

Accepting gain when it comes from another person's loss – gambling. God not only condemns unjust gain, He causes loss in the person who plays such games. Most would be shocked if they knew just how much of the world's financial system is based on gambling with the hard earned monies of others. Did you know that after we deposit our hard earned check in the bank, our banks are gambling it away in the stock market that very night? They are hoping to return it to our account by the next morning without any repercussions. Yes, that is what happens as we sleep. The bank is counting on the system of gambling (stocks) to be stable enough that we will never know our money was missing. Normally, in a healthy economy, it works; but in a failing economy, it doesn't. This is the very topic in the news as I write this. Riots are presently occurring on Wall Street because people are catching on to what I just stated. God obligates Himself to implode the system that makes money off of the losses of others. The bottom line is: there is lasting damage to any person's name (or country) that profits by the losses of other.

"How blessed is he who considers the helpless; The LORD will deliver him in a day of trouble. The LORD will protect him and keep him alive, And he shall be called blessed upon the earth; and do not give him over to the desire of his enemies" (Psalm 41:1-2).

Here are a few of the ways that we gamble:

- Lottery
- Gambling in general
- Making and selling things that hurt people
- Manipulating people into buying things they don't need
- Taking advantage of people who suffer financially
- Playing the stock market
- Etc.

Don't be late in paying those bills. Being a representative of the name of Jesus Christ reveals itself in the most practical way – that of paying our bills on time. And on those months when we simply cannot, communicate with the creditor and come up with a plan. To withhold payment is to begin the stealing process. Proverbs 3:28 tells us, "Do not say to your neighbor, 'Go, and come back, and tomorrow I will give it,' When you have it with you." If we have it, we should pay it. God always has great reasons for His order. When we withhold, it puts the lender in a position of being tempted to sin. Our actions can cause a chain reaction of sin if we don't pay our bills. When payments are late, we are telling our bill collectors that our word is worth nothing and if we are indwelt Christians – it says God's Word is worthless. " 'Then He will answer them, "Truly I say to you, to the extent that you did not do it to one of the least of these, you did not do it to Me" ' " (Matt. 25:45).

Be sure to associate and get counsel from wise people. This final requirement is probably one of the most important. Today, most Christians do not have the ability to make wise decisions. This is why we need mentors and counselors. We need guidance to make decisions that promote the name of Jesus Christ. Remember, other people will weigh the name of Jesus Christ through our actions. Sure, we end up with a "bad name"- but worse is that we give Jesus Christ a "bad name." Although, in God's reality, that is not possible; but our actions certainly do affect our Lord.

Our decisions reflect our identity. With most of us, well, let's just say we project our Savior as: a gambler, a man of debt, one who borrows and does not return what's borrowed, unjust in the marketplace, one who makes a living off of other people's losses, one who won't pay His bills on time, and one who Himself associates with unwise counsel. Wow – that is almost too much to get my brain around! What we do unto the people around us is what is done to Christ. That might be a disturbing thought to many, but it is overwhelmingly true.

It would be good of us to examine the key factors of maintaining and representing the name and reputation of Jesus Christ. To honor Christ is to know Him and to know Him is to be identified with His character.

CHAPTER 41

THE DESTRUCTION OF A GOOD NAME

Usually when we think of a man losing his reputation, or good name, we think of that man falling into immorality. Although there is a strong connection between money and immorality, in the Scriptures we find more of a focus on how a man handles his financial affairs. When I think of a man of integrity, I think of a man who does not waver under the temptation of compromise. Compromise is nothing short of settling for less than God's ideal. The not-so-funny thing about compromise is that it usually happens a little at a time. It all starts with a paper clip and gradually ends up with stealing corporate time, i.e. faking a sickness because you "needed" a little down time. Maybe you are the dishonest one who is billing for services that you don't plan to fulfill. Here is a good one: write-off personal expenses onto a corporate account, which happens to be the number one corporate abuse in America.

Compromise happens when we attempt to adjust our standards to our own pleasures. James talks about our source of quarrels and conflicts. Check this out:

"What is the source of quarrels and conflicts among you? Is not the source your pleasures that wage war in your members? You lust and do not have; so you commit murder. You are envious and cannot obtain; so you fight and quarrel. You do not have because you do not ask. You ask and do not receive, because you ask with wrong motives, so that you may spend it on your pleasures. You adulteresses, do you not know that friendship with the world is hostility toward God? Therefore whoever wishes to be a friend of the world makes himself an enemy of God" (James 4:1-4).

James just comes right out and tells us the unadulterated truth. The reason why we have conflict in our lives is because our pleasures wage war with what is right. We lust and realize what we don't have; so we compromise. The basic fact here is we are upset that we cannot obtain that "new gadget" without a compromise, so we do the very thing we hate and COMPROMISE. God wants us to see that we do not have, because we do not ask with the right motive. He loves to answer our prayers when we ask with the right motives. People asking with wrong motives are typically friends with the world. James shows us that people who have friendships with the world make themselves hostile toward God. In fact, he goes on to say that anyone who IS a friend with the world is God's enemy. Ouch!

People of compromise are revealing the evidence that their friendship with the world is much more important than their friendship with God. The world is watching "Christians" far closer than the "Christian" is willing to admit. Unbelievers are watching to determine if the so-called believer is friends with the world or not. The unsaved person's world is the world God has pressed in on them to leave. If a Christian is running into this place, why would the unsaved person want to be delivered from it? They ultimately see that the Christian is working at becoming a friend of what they have grown to hate. Well, what kind of gospel is that?

What good is there if a person (a so-called Christian) claims to have faith, but his faith is not backed by fruit? How can one be certain in Divine Truth? What is the evidence of pure and interactive faith? Faith, to some, is an intellectual assent to a religious belief system that mocks God. Is there a litmus test to find such pure faith? Could "good works" be the true and living proof of faith parted from heaven? Can a true Christian be a product of false faith?

Authentic Christianity is backed by miraculous works of Christ, which refuse to compromise. A person of compromise is functioning much like a person who is independent – "living death." The real question needing to be asked is that of independence. Since faith independent of the miraculous manifestations of Christ (Christ's works) is dead, could it be true that a person suffering with a compromising and independent spirit is revealing a "false faith?" Independent people cause suffering in the hearts of their loved ones, because they will not allow anyone to get in the way of their independence. This is why it is easy for them to compromise. People of independence find shelter and refuge in a walled fortress and refuse to let others get close to them. They find it impossible to embrace intimacy. In fact, they find more intimacy in swinging the next "deal." They tend to believe that their faith is a personal and private matter. From what we discover in the Scriptures, this is opposite of true Christianity. Even demons believe in Divine Truth, but their independence denies them Christ (James 2:19).

Could it be true that compromise along with independence is the evidence of false faith? Anyone who uses his intellectual assents, "fact faith", to prove his dedication to truth, might be in a position of mockery. But those who show their faith by the miraculous works of Christ in their day-to-day living are confessing true Salvation. If the "Tree of Knowledge of Good and Evil" is the homeland of the enemy, would it be safe to say that one of his goals is to deceive man into believing that faith is an intellectual assent? Maybe the term "intellectual assent" is too offensive? What about the knowledge of truth without the burden of proof – God's miraculous work?

Compromising people are known for justifying their actions. Justification is the act of bringing out righteousness or overlooking one's wrongs. If a person functions in a faith replicating true faith, he is demonstrating the act of bringing out his own righteousness and overlooking his own wrongs. The true test of self-justification is this: when we confront someone who has compromised, he will be quick to bear for himself internal condemnation and self-judgment – while giving the appearance of being right. If pushed, he will punish, chastise, and work to make others feel lesser than himself. A person of compromise usually suffers with a lifestyle of guilt and hidden condemnation. He has moments of truth versus a life of truth. He lies, covers up, and deceives others into thinking he is doing well. Yet all the while, he is falling into a dark hole of self-judgment, typically resulting in a bad reputation.

CHAPTER 42

THE BUILDING BLOCKS OF A GOOD NAME

Praying for a good name is the starting place for a good name. But before we put our building blocks in place, let us examine authentic justification, sanctification, and faith.

The term "true justification through Christ" is much different than how most self-proclaimed Christians use it. The actual definition of justification is that of the illustration of Passover – forgiveness. Compromising, independent people try to forgive themselves without the appropriation of Christ's redemptive justification or try to live up to a reputation they themselves put in place. Justification is a gift and it comes to us through grace, a freewill offering from Christ. It means to "remove one's sins from someone." It is noted in the Greek text as "remission." Remission is the process of restarting or being given a second chance at His mission. In order for this to happen, one's sins must be put aside or "sent away." The Hebrew text reveals to us an even clearer understanding of this: "to place on the side, to disregard or bypass." In the Old Testament, man's sins were removed, or passed over, until the next animal sacrifice took place. The "sinners'" sins were placed on the animal and it was killed in order to send the sins away. This is why Jesus had to become a permanent sacrifice for all sin – to permanently provide a pass over of all past, present, and future sins. The Old Testament's version of sacrifice did not change the heart or character of man; it simply, temporarily removed the sin itself. The New Covenant (the blood sacrifice of Jesus) removed sin and its power, as well as, guilt. Jesus' blood sacrifice also changed the identity and heart of the man. In short, He made us just – just as if we did not sin.

People with compromising reputations are not only independent, but they tend to mock God by attempting to accomplish more faith, or prove their faith, by expecting fruit just because they have obtained faith. In reality, faith is not accompanied by its inevitable and expectant fruits. True faith is alive, active, and mixed with the love of God, which produces good works.

Compromising people of a bad reputation profess and presume faith. The end result is a barren and destitute tree that cannot produce fruit. Even demons have this kind of faith. This type of "false faith" consists of the intellectual belief of sin and the work of Christ, instead of repenting and returning to God to rely on His promises. Independents usually focus on getting themselves bailed out of selfish behavior or use God's promises to prosper themselves. They lean toward treating God like He is some type of slot machine. When works are practiced instead of being a result of faith, they are false works, producing plastic fruit.

Can non-Christians produce real fruit? This question demands an answer with a question. Can pine trees produce apples? Of course not! This is one of the toughest doctrines for Christians and non-Christians alike to embrace. All the "good works" of unsaved people do nothing. They may see temporary benefits here on earth, but the eternal value is useless (James 2:20). Unsaved people are in need of new life. They need to ask the Lord Jesus to come and dwell within their mortal bodies. This process is called being born-again. Once a person asks Christ into his life, the Holy Spirit comes to live within him. This process of sanctification converts him into a "fruit tree." Now the life of Christ, through the seed of faith (Matt. 17:20) that He places in the new believer, can begin producing real fruit – love, joy, peace, patience, kindness, goodness, faithfulness, gentleness, and self-control (Gal. 5:22-23).

Can Christians be a part of "false faith?" One of the greatest controversies of Christianity is that of "sinless perfection." A Christian never becomes sinless because of the sin that remains within the mortal body of the believer. Sin means "to miss the mark." All Christians have the choice to sin, even though they are perfect spiritually in Christ Jesus. Even the most obedient Christian cannot say that he has not sinned as a believer. "Therefore, to one who knows the right thing to do and does not do it, to him it is sin" (James 4:17). No Christian can keep all the mandates of God, nor does He expect us to. This is why He sent His Son to fulfill the law in and through us.

Once we accept Christ into our lives, we are given a new nature, a new reputation – the nature of Christ Himself. This reputation comes with a new past – the past of Jesus Christ Himself. True authentic Christianity comes with a brand new reputation; a reputation, I might add, that is NOT earned, worked at, or acted out. His reputation is given to us as a gift. This is accomplished by God sending the Holy Spirit to live within our mortal bodies. The doctrines of perfection come into play when the Spirit purifies our spiritual nature, which is what becomes perfect in Christ. The mind and body remain vulnerable to our "flesh" (the trash the old man left behind) because sin continues to reside in our bodies and persists in affecting our minds. We are given the power to resist indwelling sin (our old reputation) and choose life coming through our new spiritual nature. This is why we are called to "put off the old self and put on the new" (Eph. 4:22). When sin, flesh, decides to raise its ugly head through the body (Rom. 7:23) by way of the mind, we are to "consider ourselves dead to sin and our old reputation, but alive to God in Christ Jesus" and His reputation (Rom. 6:11).

CHAPTER 43

THE MASTERMIND OF REPUTATIONS

"For I joyfully concur with the law of God in the inner man, but I see a different law in the members of my body, waging war against the law of my mind and making me a prisoner of the law of sin which is in my members" (Rom. 7:22-23).

The mind is "grand central station" for the function and appropriation of what man believes. It is like the hard drive on a computer: whatever gets programmed in, is the instruction the system uses to carry out orders. The mind IS renewable – thank God. When we were unsaved, the sin nature was controlled and mastered by Satan himself. He was the sole programmer of our little hard drive – called the mind of man. Once we became saved, we were given a new Master (programmer) – Christ, through the power of the indwelling Spirit. Knowing this, we are given the mandate to choose to submit to our new Master programmer. In our unsaved state, the master programmer was Satan. Once Christ came, He removed the old programmer and placed Himself at the keyboard. But, the data the enemy placed on our hard drives (mind and body) remains and is in need of being renewed (2 Cor. 4:16). This is the process that the Bible calls "working out your Salvation." It is a daily, moment by moment process that brings us freedom from the enslaving issues left behind by the old programmer.

Now, let's address the issue of Christians living in "false faith." When children of God choose to sin, willfully or not, communion with God is interrupted and the fruit of the Spirit cease to flow. After this occurs, the Christian has the prerogative of "faking it until he makes it" OR repenting and reestablishing the overflow from the indwelling Spirit. If the believer chooses not to repent, the sin(s) become habitual and the believer typically begins to use his faith to produce plastic fruit – fruit unto death (Rom. 7:5). This is what develops the independence in the believer. He chooses to allow the flesh to have temporary mastery, which God has judged and set aside forever. Many believers are simply ignorant of this truth.

The unsaved man sins out of his sinful nature; whereas when a Christian chooses to sin, he sins directly against God. Since God has given His children the power not to sin, it becomes grievous to God when one of His children chooses to sin anyway. But, when non-Christians sin, it is the enemy who sins directly against God. The unsaved man has no choice but to sin, it is who he is! The unbeliever is judged by the law, because he is under the law. The Christian is judged by grace, because he is under the law of the Spirit of life (Rom. 8:2).

When a believer sins, he places himself under the correction and governmental dealings of God. When his sin is confessed, the believer is responding to earthly, self-judgment. He is then able to appropriate his forgiveness offered through the life of Christ. Keep in mind that the forgiveness is already complete, but it needs to be appropriated by the born-again believer. Communion is oneness and oneness exists in our Spirit, but our souls can detach from the experience of oneness. This is why we just need to be honest with Christ within us, take ownership of the sin we committed, and begin enjoying communion that is already made available for us to enjoy. But, there is a leading factor that needs to be considered. God oftentimes allows the temporal consequences of a person's wrongdoing through earthly bodily suffering, circumstances, or lifestyle changes. If the Christian continues in willful sin, darkness (which is characteristic of unbelief) controls the heart. Fake faith and reputation become inevitable and the believer most assuredly will come under the corrective hand of God (Acts 5:1-16; 1 Cor. 11:28-32).

One of the most challenging individuals to deal with is the so-called "believer" who says he has had a salvation experience, but reverts back to the world, and by all obvious signs, stays there. This is the group of people " 'who, when they hear, receive the word with joy; and these have no firm root; they believe for a while, and in time of temptation fall away' " (Luke 8:13). The word "believe" is not to be associated with true faith in Jesus, which transforms the person from the inside out. But rather, this type of belief is that of an intellectual assent. This person does not display the type of repentance that leads to godliness, but only to regret (2 Cor. 7:10). These "believers" do not hate sin, but rather promote it. They return to their sin like a dog to their vomit (2 Peter 2:19-22). He makes a firm stand on his "faith" in Christ, but does not profess Him with his works. Like the washing of a pig externally, this person may appear to change, but that change then disappears. This is evidence there has been no change of nature or disposition – he is still lacking in true Salvation.

There is yet another type of "believer" - the one who knows and chooses a life of unbelief. This person is willfully choosing not to believe in the message of Truth. He is dead to Christ, alive to the enemy, and will suffer the same consequences God has reserved for Satan himself.

As for those Christians who speak and act, as those who are to be judged by the law of liberty, we still have a judgment to face. James tells us that the believer is going to be judged by the liberality and generosity of Christ Himself. Our judgment will be proportionate to the amount of mercy we have shown here on earth. For those who showed no mercy, they will receive no mercy. The entrance into heaven is a result of the work of Christ, but the enjoyment of heaven and its rewards will be proportionate to what the believer did for Christ in his life of faith on earth. This is a reality that Christians rarely talk about (James 2:12-13).

In conclusion, a man is justified (just as if he did not sin) by applying the works of Christ in Himself, and not by faith alone. Just like the body without the spirit is dead, so also is faith without its best friend, faith (James 2:24, 26). Jesus said that the world would know us by our fruit and fruit comes as a result of works being blended with faith. Faith starts by believing God, without having to have all the answers first. Works should be a spontaneous act, resulting from believing in the substance of things hoped for. If I remember correctly, works and faith mixed together make a solid reputation!

CHAPTER 44

PRAYER & THE LOVE OF MONEY

Before we appeal to the Lord for more money, there are a few things we must keep in mind about prayer. Satan has successfully used the world, and all of its influences, to bring a lighthearted attitude and mindset regarding the kingdom of darkness. Just take a look at the enormous volume of books, movies, video games, T-shirts, music, toys, television, advertisements, the internet, fashions, jewelry, and of course, silly jesting we are bombarded with wherever we turn!

The desensitization about Satan and his role in man's sin is a subtle, but strategic attack on God's divine creation – His blessed children. The enemy of this world sees to it that the world (his domain) laughs him off with indifference. Always remember that this callousness is the most powerful tool the enemy has in defusing God's serious plan of redemption. Christians ought never to entertain crude joke making, purchase degrading media products, or lightheartedly support Satan in any way. Believers need to exercise care in not assigning all of their wrongdoing as Satan's responsibility. We must, with biblical insight, understand the limited power of Satan and his kingdom. Oppression and bondage is not a joking matter.

The key in the believer's emphasis on biblical prayer must be based on a biblical approach to the subject. Subjective feelings, emotional desires, and fervent sincerity are not sufficient weaponry against an enemy who laughs in the face of our intents. He yields no ground to emotion or sincerity. He retreats only from the authority and power that has been given to the Christian through his/her union with the Lord Jesus Christ and the absolute Truth of the Word of God. An illustration worth remembering is this: If I were to give you a sharp two-edged sword and a butter knife, which would you use to fight an assailant? Dumb question? I don't think so! Your logical mind would choose the sharp two-edged sword.

However, in reality, when we do not use the Word of God to fight off the enemy, we are essentially using a butter knife to war against an enemy who slings a ball and chain.

"Take . . . the sword of the Spirit, which is the word of God" (Eph. 6:17b).

We have two basic offensive weapons to use against Satan. They are the Word of God and the power of prayer. When we put the two of these together, we have the most intimidating weapon known to the enemy. He knows he has "been had" when a man of God masters the art of using the Word of God in the power of prayer.

I pray that you are beginning to see our critical need for the Word of God and prayer. The sword of the Spirit, God's Word, is living and active. These are not just words on a page. They are life-giving Words from the mouth of a living God! Use our words and we die. Use God's Words, we live. It's as simple as that!

"For the word of God is living and active and sharper than any two-edged sword, and piercing as far as the division of soul and spirit, of both joints and marrow, and able to judge the thoughts and intentions of the heart" (Heb. 4:12).

The Word is eternal, just as God Himself is eternal. Just as God is omnipotent (all-powerful), so does His Word have all the needed power to defeat the enemy and to accomplish God's will. Just as God is immutable, so the Word of God will never change. Just as our Lord is omnipresent, so His Word is always there and ready to be used in every situation. Just as God is Holy, so His Word is Holy. The bottom line is this: His Word is living, active, and sharper than any two-edged sword. The enemy hates hearing it. Jesus used it to fight off temptation. We can't survive without it.

As a sword, the Word has the power to penetrate the life of every being who hears it, including the enemy. It is meant to do corrective surgery within the soul, spirit, thoughts, attitudes, and body of all who hear it. This is the secret of its power against the enemy. The Word can penetrate, cleanse, and change the life of those who embrace it as Truth. This is why it cuts away at the grip of the enemy. There is nothing more powerful (and certainly no substitute) for persistent, steady, consistent application of coming against the enemy. Even Jesus, the Son of God, used the written Word in the wilderness to fight off Satan. What worked for the Son of the living God will certainly do no less for us!

"Jesus, full of the Holy Spirit, returned from the Jordan and was led around by the Spirit in the wilderness for forty days being tempted by the devil. And He ate nothing during those days, and when they had ended, He became hungry. And the devil said to Him, 'If You are the Son of God, tell this stone to become bread' " (Luke 4:1-3).

The importance of doctrinal Truth and doctrinal praying is given to us by God to use daily. Doctrine, God's unchanging Truth, is mighty in defeating our enemies. As Christians, this Truth must go deep into our hearts. This can only come about as we gain understanding of the Holy Word of God and then use that Word aggressively in our lives.

Normally speaking, I am not one who advocates following "steps" to embrace freedom. However, when it comes to deliverance from strongholds in our lives, I see a definite need for a plan to faithfully follow these suggestions word for word; they will equip us and build a foundation for our soul. The Holy Spirit will aggressively act to guard our heart against our enemies.

WARNING

Whenever we go to the front lines, where the enemy lives and breathes, he is bound to try chasing us away. We must not submit to his deceptive ideas and lies that tell us: there is no time, this level of combat isn't necessary; these are "only" words; we can put this off because we already have too many things to do; we're too tired, or too sick; or we are already struggling with worries, doubts, and fears which will prevent us from completing our pathway to deliverance. We need to push through it all and respond like warriors!

In rare cases, some people experience terrifying feelings of guilt, worthlessness, physical symptoms (choking, pains moving around their body, tightness above the eyes, dizziness, blackouts, or even fainting) and terrifying spells of panic and/or depression. Remember, fear is the fire of the dragon's mouth – it is his primary tool of intimidation. Don't worry – it's only hot air!

Another warning: avoid becoming preoccupied with Satan and his domain. Have you ever wondered why people are intrigued with movies, video games, and music based on the dark side? One of the games the enemy plays is to create an unhealthy fascination with his work. Many people are caught up in giving more attention and credit to the enemy than they do God. I call this a "demon behind every bush" mentality. It is common for those who are struggling with satanic affliction to be preoccupied with the enemy due to their level of temptation, obsession, and negative thoughts. However, we must take special caution to keep our eyes upon Jesus. Well-trained Christians in the Word and Spirit will not fear Satan or his schemes.

The Christian is engaged in a spiritual battle, even if he does not believe that he is. Satan and his spiritual forces are on the battle line waiting for us each day. Man does not have a choice as to his engagement in this battle. It awaits him each day and there is no way of getting around it. If you are saved and have received Jesus Christ as your Lord and Savior, you are in! Be alert and sober, for your enemy (Satan) roams around on the earth to seek whom he can devour (1 Peter 5:8). Are you battle ready? SEE YOU ON THE FRONT LINES!

Biblical doctrines and money have much in common. To avoid the root of all evil (the love of money), or should I say, the root of Satan, we must have an honest, biblical view of money and prayer.

CHAPTER 45

POWER OF MONEY & PRAYER

God says the rain falls on the just and the unjust. For our reading benefit, we could easily say the "money falls on the just and the unjust." I cannot tell you how many times I have heard a believer ask, "Why is it that God allows the ungodly to prosper while Christians suffer with little?" The answer is found in reviewing the end-times. The way one spoils a rich kid is by allowing him to get sick from spoiling himself. As we look around at the end-times, we see an entire world prospering, but only for a season. As with all spoiled children, people of the world only focus on others to get what they want, in order to spend it on their own pleasures.

"You ask and do not receive, because you ask with wrong motives, so that you may spend it on your pleasures" (James 4:3)

Typically, God avoids supporting anything that gets in the way of true dependence on Him. Money has a way of leading people away from God, NOT to Him. God uses all things to lead each of His children to call out to Him – not, his banker. Believers are being awakened to the reality that their fight in life is not against flesh and blood, but the powers of darkness and the principalities of the air (Eph. 6:12). So many Christians today are deceived into thinking that what they see is what they are to battle. As the Lord draws near, we can be assured that our battle with the world, the flesh, and the devil will intensify. Worldly ideas of pop psychology will increase as the primary solution to our troubled minds. More rapidly than most of us realize, the questions people ask are based on worldly fables called philosophies of man. God is calling each of His children to call upon Him and He will deliver according to His divine Truth and Will.

Fear of confronting the enemy has held most believers back from boldly going before the throne of God regarding the temptations and afflictions of the enemy. God's greatest servants have always shared an appreciation of the magnificent power of prayer and the complete victory over Satan's kingdom available to all believers, through the mighty Person and work of our Husband, Jesus Christ.

The book of Ephesians is the New Testament handbook on spiritual, biblical prayer. Get to know this book like a handbook. The believer's emphasis in prayer must be upon a biblical and sound doctrinal approach to this subject. The Word of God recognizes that we encounter the three faces of Satan—the world, the flesh, and the devil. When a person becomes born-again, his/her relationship to everything in the physical, spiritual, mental, and emotional world completely changes. Since the believer is a citizen of heaven, he is given the power to face the enemy toe-to-toe. Scary? Well, look at it this way. Either we face him head-on or he will constantly be nipping at our heel—eating away our lives a little at a time.

To resist the limited power of the enemy, one must submit therefore to God first, then resist the evil one and he will flee. It is a promise given to us by God (James 4:7).

Because of our newly found relationship with God, all believers are marked targets for attack from God's enemy—Satan. Where does he seem to attack first? The love of money, of course! Since the love of money is the root of Satan, I would think this would be his main area of attack. If he can get the Bride of Christ to love money more than her Husband, believers will then begin to worship money and ultimately, Satan – a simple scam from a complex enemy.

Understanding that he is relentless in his attacks, believers must embrace the truth that the Father has given them a defense system—the power of prayer.

First things first, we must not depend upon feeling and experience as an evidence of our being strong enough to pray. The power and ability to pray boldly is to be based upon objective fact and not upon subjective feelings. The power of prayer is to be appropriated by faith and faith alone. The following are Four Phases of Effectual Prayers:

1. Personal Reflection and Confession
2. Praise and Adoration
3. Prayers of Supplication
4. Worship and Affirmation

PERSONAL REFLECTION & CONFESSION

The following outline presents a biblical procedure for your, and my, personal reflection and confession time with the Lord.

- Engage in an honest appraisal regarding your selfishness. It is important to be open and honest with God about yourself.
- Confess all known sin (1 John 1:9). Verbalize your sins against yourself and others. Confessions take back from Satan any ground which he has taken from you.
- Extend forgiveness to those who have hurt you. Unforgiveness is the primary reason most Christians don't pray consistently. List out who hurt you, how they hurt you, and your reaction. Bring the offender and how they hurt you before Him and extend forgiveness to them in prayer. Now confess to God that your reactions to these offenses are sin, accept His forgiveness, and tell Him you are willing to seek the offender's forgiveness for those reactions.
- Yield yourself to God (Rom. 6:13). As an act of your will (displace your feelings), yield all areas of your life to Him—spiritual, psychological, physical, social, marital, parental, and financial.
- Express your passion and desire for the Holy Spirit to renew your mind.
- Believe with your mind that the Holy Spirit will fill you up with His power—remember to set your "feelings" aside and claim this by faith.
- Now obey God in all that He reveals and expresses in the Scriptures and begin to pray doctrinally.

PRAISE & ADORATION

Walking after the Spirit is absolutely essential if we are to bring praise and adoration before the Father. When God said to enter the courtyard with thanksgiving and prayer, He was quite serious. That means in richness and poverty. We must learn to "abase and abound" as an equal gift from God. Many Christians attempt to praise God while having "things" in their lives they are not thankful for. Philippians 4:6 says: "Be anxious for nothing, but in everything by prayer and supplication with thanksgiving let your requests be made known to God." It is difficult, if not impossible, to pray and supplicate with anxiety in one's heart. The way to remove anxious thoughts is through thanksgiving! "In Him, you also, after listening to the message of truth, the gospel of your salvation—having also believed, you were sealed in Him with the Holy Spirit of promise, who is given as a pledge of our inheritance, with a view to the redemption of God's own possession, to the praise of His glory" (Eph. 1:13-14). Thanksgiving and praise for what He has accomplished for us through the Holy Spirit of promise is enough to be thankful for in spite of our infirmities. Prayers of praise and adoration are simply admiring the Person and work of God no matter what circumstance we are faced with. It is crucial to acknowledge before God that we are grateful for all things, before we petition for all things.

PRAYERS & SUPPLICATIONS

Intercessory prayer is the practice of praying or applying the objective, absolute Truths of the Word of God as the hope and basis of resolving our prayer burden. God loves for us to pray His Word back to Him - claiming His attributes, promises and redemptive work as the foundation of our faith and hope that He will answer our supplications. The hope and solution of the prayer burden, however, is always based upon the objective absolutes of God's attributes and character as revealed in His Holy Word.

Experienced prayer warriors know that using their own ideas, or words, accomplishes nothing; but by using the Word of God in prayers, the enemy shutters and backs down. He, the enemy, cannot stand when the Word is used to combat the elements of his doings. Quoting verses while praying is what puts the enemy in his place—dark places. When we attempt to confront the tactics of our foe by using our own sincerity and efforts, we will soon discover he is not intimidated by us or our efforts. Doctrinal praying should occupy much of our daily prayer time. It must be used in praise, petition, and intercession. Herein, lies one of God's greatest gifts to us for our prayer times.

Believers have a supernatural resource of wealth and riches in the grace and gifts bestowed upon us in the Lord Jesus Christ. The Truths are ours for claiming power, position, authority, and total victory over Satan's world, which actually belongs to God the Father. The believer's victory over the enemy is absolute when the enemy attempts to use God's Truth to defeat us—his primary tactic of deception.

"For though we walk in the flesh, we do not war according to the flesh, for the weapons of our warfare are not of the flesh, but divinely powerful for the destruction of fortresses. We are destroying speculations and every lofty thing raised up against the knowledge of God, and we are taking every thought captive to the obedience of Christ" (2 Cor. 10:3-5).

It is important we learn to pray aggressive biblical prayers for family and friends who we believe are struggling with the bondage of the love of money. Pray this prayer aloud when led to intercede for an individual.

SAMPLE INTERCESSORY PRAYER FOR MONEY BONDAGE

My dear heavenly Father, in the name of our Lord Jesus Christ,
I bring myself before You and ask for the Holy Spirit's guidance that I might pray in the Spirit as You have taught me. I thank You, Father, that You have sovereign control over all my money or lack of it. I thank You for the level of material possessions that you have placed in my life. In the name of the Lord Jesus and as a priest of God, I ask for mercy and forgiveness for the sins of the love of money, which grieve You. I plead the sufficiency of the blood of Christ to meet the full penalty that my sins deserve. I claim back the ground I have yielded to the enemy in my life, which I have knowingly, or unknowingly, given to Satan by believing the enemy's deception. In the name of the Lord Jesus Christ, I resist all of Satan's activity to use Your money or possessions that You entrusted to me. Exercising my authority, which is given to me in my union with the Lord Jesus Christ, I pull down the strongholds which the kingdom of darkness has formed against me with the love of money. I smash, break, and destroy all those plans formed against my mind, will, emotions, and

even my wallet. I destroy in prayer the spiritual blindness and deafness that Satan has perpetrated against me.

I invite the Holy Spirit of God to bring the fullness of His power to convict, to bring to repentance, and to lead me into faith in the Lord Jesus Christ – my Savior. I cover myself with the blood of the Lord Jesus Christ and I break Satan's power to blind me to the Truth of God.

I believe that You, Jesus Christ, and the Holy Spirit are leading me to claim my freedom in You and I thank You for the answer to my prayer. In the name of Jesus, I joyfully lay this prayer before You in the worthiness of His completed work. Amen.

CHAPTER 46

PRAYING FOR MORE MONEY

My family has been living on "missionary support" off and (more) "on" since 1980, when I went on staff at Grace Fellowship International in Denver. We have become so dependent upon the Lord for our food, gas, clothing, and lodging that it has almost become a way of life. You would think that this would be a great benefit and become easy after all these years – BUT, it has not. Depending on God never gets easier. In fact, our experience is that the longer we live on missionary support, the harder it gets, because we struggle with the issue of man being our provider vs. God Himself.

God blesses the just and the unjust with prosperity to a certain degree. Remember when He said:

" 'But I say to you, love your enemies and pray for those who persecute you, so that you may be sons of your Father who is in heaven; for He causes His sun to rise on the evil and the good, and sends rain on the righteous and the unrighteous' " (Matt. 5:44-45).

Before praying for money, food, and lodging and expecting a response, we have to be an indwelt born-again Christian. God does not answer the prayers of unsaved people – unless it is a prayer of Salvation. If He did – He would be prospering their way to hell. We don't serve a God who rewards demonic, good flesh. God hears the petitions of His babies, the Bridal members of His Son. If you're not saved, you have no mediator to deliver your prayers unto the Father – plain and simple. The first thing an unbeliever should ask for is the Holy Spirit!

" 'If you then, being evil, know how to give good gifts to your children, how much more will your heavenly Father give the Holy Spirit to those who ask Him?' " (Luke 11:13).

You and I have heard hundreds of unsaved people pray over food, sick children, and even plead to God for money. Does God hear their prayers? The odds are – yes. But He will not give unto an evil dweller. All unsaved people are evil dwellers – that is why they go to hell. The reason why the Emergent movement is so acceptable and popular is because these groups of "self-proclaimed Christians" allow unbelievers to pray like children of God. It confuses the pathway to Salvation and it robs them of the need to beg for Salvation and Deliverance.

We become children of God, members of God's holy family, by faith in Christ Jesus. This cannot happen without a truckload of trust in the Lord Jesus Christ. Trust is not going to manifest until we are broken and crucified with Christ – which is our personal Salvation. Only then, do we have the privilege to pray and expect God to give us His answer.

Secondly, once we know we are truly indwelt by the Holy Spirit (saved), we must pray with the right motive. Most prayers that I hear come out of the mouths of believers are so they can spend on their own pleasures or because they don't want to suffer with their particular thorn.

"You ask and do not receive, because you ask with wrong motives, so that you may spend it on your pleasures" (James 4:3).

If we were to be truly honest, most of our prayers are for selfish motives or minimally, to stop the suffering of another loved one. How often do you hear Christians pray to be well content with problems, adversity, or being hurt by another? After being a counselor for 30 plus years – I can say that I know few.

"Therefore I am well content with weaknesses, with insults, with distresses, with persecutions, with difficulties, for Christ's sake; for when I am weak, then I am strong" (2 Cor. 12:10).

How in God's name was Paul able to pray such a prayer? Aren't we supposed to pray against weaknesses, insults from others, stress in our lives, and certainly against pain inflicted upon us by others? The answer is NO! Paul was so troubled by this "thorn" in his flesh that he appealed to the Lord "three" times that it would part from him. First of all, the "it" is a demonic being. Check this out:

"Because of the surpassing greatness of the revelations, for this reason, to keep me from exalting myself, there was given me a thorn in the flesh, a messenger of Satan to torment me--to keep me from exalting myself!" (2 Cor. 12:7).

The Greek for "messenger of Satan" translates out as "worker of the abyss, which translates in the English as – demon. It was a demon sanding the edges of Paul's flesh – buffeting him. The most interesting note here, at least for me, is that Paul only appealed to the Lord "three" times. That means he only brought it up in his prayer life before God three times throughout his entire service to the Lord. Most indwelt Christians pray about harassments like these three times an hour. I certainly have! Not Paul; we learn from the Scriptures, he was such a man of faith that he typically spoke to God and believed God would answer according to His Divine manner. Paul was so known for being a man of faith that the demonic world knew him right along with Jesus.

"And the evil spirit answered and said to them, 'I recognize Jesus, and I know about Paul, but who are you?' " (Acts 19:15).

Are you known by the spirit world like Paul and Jesus? How does one gain such a status? Easy – ask once and trust in God for His time and answer. That is what faith is! Badgering God like some kind of spoiled child is not faith. Don't get me wrong, you can badger God and He will still love you. But don't expect Him to "kowtow" to your appeal. The truth of the matter is – we all do this from time to time – even Paul. Now mind you, he only asked three times for a particular thorn that just happened to affect his daily living, but that still was outside of his norm. He was really hurting! Did God take this thorn in his flesh, "messenger of Satan," from Paul? No, I am afraid He didn't! In fact, this was such a significant moment for Paul, Jesus showed up personally 60 years after He ascended. What does He say to Paul?

"And He has said to me, 'My grace is sufficient for you, for power is perfected in weakness.' Most gladly, therefore, I will rather boast about my weaknesses, so that the power of Christ may dwell in me" (2 Cor. 12:9).

Let's get this straight. Paul asks a simple request to be relieved from some pain and suffering and Jesus comes back with "My grace is sufficient?" Then Jesus has the boldness to go on and say that "power is perfected in weakness." Wow! I would think that if any human deserved a little relief, it would be Paul. BUT no, he is asked to embrace his weakness. The reason why Paul was able to say he is "well content" with the very thing he was asking Christ to remove was because he accepted the simple one liner "My grace is sufficient for you, for power is perfected in weakness."

Self-proclaimed Christians today have been trained to stand against Satan and rebuke all their infirmities. Many times I really do wonder whom they are really rebuking. Is it really Satan they are coming against? Would that "name it and claim it" theology have worked for Paul? I think the answer should be obvious.

Let's face it – we live in a generation that treats God like He is some kind of "sugar daddy." We have been duped by the enemy to rebuke him, when in reality we are coming against the sovereign doctrines of God – if not God Himself. When we ask of the Father, it is critical we ask with the right motives and not to have it benefit ourselves. We should be willing to suffer for the sake of other people's sins, just as Christ did. If Christ truly does live in us, then isn't it feasible that He would still want to do that through us? If you are a believer of the Exchanged Life – the answer is yes!

Another critical factor is that when we pray, we must pray based on the name of Jesus Christ. Praying in one's identity is just as important as praying with the right motive. When Jesus asked us to pray in His name, He was saying to pray in our identity in Christ. From our identity we find motives and without Christ as Life identity, we have wrong motives. Therefore, the reason why we have so many self-life prayers in the world today is because they do not understand their identity (name) in Christ. Character, behavior, and function come from one's view of his identity. This is why self-proclaimed Christians pray for God to bless ridiculous things like divorces and dishonest gain - all in the name of "God wants me to be happy." Really? Try to sell that one to Paul, Peter, and all the rest of the disciples who died a martyr's death. What has happened to Christ's Church (true believers)? This, I can say - The body of Christ is a long distance away from knowing who she is in Christ. And the body of Christ will continue to ask for things from God in order to spend it on her own pleasures. She will go on quarreling/having conflicts/ waging war with her own flesh, lusting, and being upset because she does not have what her neighbors enjoy. I am not trying to be a downer here, but the Church has become friends with the world and does not realize that those who become friends with the world and its pleasures – become an enemy of God. In fact, she is setting up a hostile relationship with God.

"You adulteresses, do you not know that friendship with the world is hostility toward God? Therefore whoever wishes to be a friend of the world makes himself an enemy of God" (James 4:4).

One of the greatest dangers of a Christian's prayer life is praying for worldly things. Not to say we can't, but one must be very careful. Praying for material things, including money, needs to be for the Divine purpose of progressing the kingdom of God. Yes, nice homes, cars, and even jewelry can actually be used to glorify God. But realistically, I have met few who can find that balance.

Let us commit to praying for one another to stay focused on asking with righteous motives – for all of us can fall into the temptation of asking God for money, things, and healings that are not of the Lord's Divine calling.

APPENDIX:
(Prayers/Scriptures)

Salvation

Loving heavenly Father, I take by faith the helmet of Salvation. I recognize that my Salvation is in the Person of Your Son, the Lord Jesus Christ. I cover my mind with His; I desire that He put His mind within me. Let my thoughts be His thoughts. I open my mind fully and only to the control of the Lord Jesus Christ. I replace my own selfish and sinful thoughts with His. I reject every projected thought of Satan and his demons and instead, I request the mind of the Lord Jesus Christ. Grant me the wisdom to discern thoughts that are from the world, my old sin nature, and Satan's kingdom.

I believe: Jesus is Your Son, He died on the Cross for my sins, and Jesus is God. I believe in: the Trinity; You, as the Father; Jesus, as the Son; and the Holy Spirit. I confess that I have been a sinner – totally separated from You. I choose to accept Your forgiveness for my sins through the power of the blood of Jesus that was shed for me on the Cross. I now ask that you send the Holy Spirit to live inside my mortal body. (Pause for a moment)

I praise You, heavenly Father, that I may know the mind of Christ as I hide Your Word within my heart and mind. Open my heart to love Your Word. Grant to me the ability and capacity to memorize large portions of it. May Your Word be ever over my mind like a helmet of strength, which Satan's projected thoughts cannot penetrate. Cause me to allow the Holy Spirit (the Life of Christ) within me to fulfill the discipline of daily living to appropriate Your Salvation. These things I lay before You in the precious name of my new Savior, the Lord Jesus Christ. Amen!

Self-Life Prayer

I hereby surrender everything that I am, and have, and ever will be. I take my hands off of my life and release every relationship to You: every habit, every goal, my health, my wealth, and everything that means anything. I surrender it ALL to

You. By faith I take my place at the Cross, believing that when the Lord Jesus was crucified, according to Your Word, I was crucified with Him; when He was buried, I was buried; when He was raised from the dead, I was raised with Him. I deny myself the right to rule and reign in my own life and I take up the Cross believing that I was raised from the dead and seated at Your right hand.

I thank You for saving me from my sins and myself. From this moment on I am trusting You to live Your life in me and through me, instead of me; to do what I can't do; quit what I can't quit; start what I can't start; and--most of all--to be what I can't be. I am trusting you to renew my mind and heal damaged emotions in Your time. I thank You now by faith for accepting me in the Lord Jesus, for giving me Your grace, Your freedom, Your joy, Your victory and Your righteousness as my inheritance. Even if I don't feel anything, I know that Your Word is true; I am counting on Your Spirit to do what Your Word says-- to set me free from myself, that Your resurrection life may be lived out through me, and that You may receive all the glory.

I thank You and praise You for victory right now in Jesus' name, Amen.

Stewardship

Matthew 6:20-21

"But store up for yourselves treasures in heaven, where neither moth nor rust destroys, and where thieves do not break in or steal; for where your treasure is, there your heart will be also."

Matthew 6:33

"But seek first His kingdom and His righteousness, and all these things will be added to you."

Matthew 19:29

"And everyone who has left houses or brothers or sisters or father or mother or children or farms for My name's sake, will receive many times as much, and will inherit eternal life."

Luke 6:38

"Give, and it will be given to you. They will pour into your lap a good measure-- pressed down, shaken together, and running over. For by your standard of measure it will be measured to you in return."

1 Corinthians 16:1-2

Now concerning the collection for the saints, as I directed the churches of Galatia, so do you also. On the first day of every week each one of you is to put aside and save, as he may prosper, so that no collections be made when I come.

2 Corinthians 9:6-8

Now this I say, he who sows sparingly will also reap sparingly, and he who sows bountifully will also reap bountifully. Each one must do just as he has purposed in his heart, not grudgingly or under compulsion, for God loves a cheerful giver. And God is able to make all grace abound to you, so that always having all sufficiency in everything, you may have an abundance for every good deed.

ABOUT THE AUTHOR:

Dr. Phinney is the Founder and Ministry Host of the Institute Of Ministry (IOM America) and founder to the Exchanged Life Global Initiative, as well as the International Fellowship of Exchanged Life (IFEL). Stephen is also the co-founder of the Men Mapping Outreach Ministries, a ministry dedicated to equipping men to be protectors of women, children, community, and nation.

Stephen has authored multiple books/teaching series on spiritual growth and has published over 200 online articles/booklets assisting others in obtaining a Transformational Biblical Worldview. Even though he does NOT put much stock in these degrees, he holds a Bachelor's degree in Psychology, Masters in Counseling Psychology, and a Doctorate in Ministry. He also holds the status of Doctor of Philosophy Candidate at Oxford Graduate School.

OBJECTIVE:
Phinney's primary objective is to equip individuals for the purpose of building up the Body of Christ and assist in empowering men, women, children, and family units to have a generational impact on the communities they serve. This is accomplished by providing training, mentorship, and counseling by making use of the believer's identity in Christ.

FAMILY:
Stephen & Jane have been married for over 35 years and have three grown children: Abigail (husband, Quintin Eason), Elizabeth (husband, Nathan Ford) and Jessica. Jane & Steve have also been blessed with seven grandchildren. They are dedicated to the institution of marriage, multigenerational family development, and local multigenerational family church development. They are conference speakers on topics relating to core marriage, multigenerational family, leadership values, and the Exchanged Life (Not I, but Christ).

BIBLIOGRAPHY:

- † **Scripture** taken from the New American Standard Bible, © Copyright 1960, 1962, 1963, 1968, 1971, 1972, 1973, 1975, 1977, 1995 by The Lockman Foundation. Used by permission.
- † **God's Miraculous Plan of Economy**, Taylor: Jack, Broadman Press, 1975
- † **The Coming Economic Armageddon**, Jeremiah: David, Faith Words, 2008
- † **The Revelation**, Greene: Oliver, The Gospel Hour, 1963
- † **Epicenter**, Rosenberg: Joel, Tyndale, 2006
- † **The Revolution**, Rosenberg: Joel, Tyndale, 2009
- † **Money Talks and So Can We**, Blue: Ron, Zondervan Publishing House, 1999
- † **Because The Time Is Near**, MaCarthur: John, Moody Publishers, 2007
- † **Revelation**, MaCarthur: John, Moody Publishers, 2000
- † **Crown Ministries**, 2009
- † **God's War on Terror**, Shoebat: Walid, Richardson: Joel, Executive Media, 2008
- † **Governance Matters**, Stahlke: Les, Imperial, 2003
- † **The Two Babylons**, Hislop: Alexander, Loizeaux Brothers, 1916
- † **The Adversary**, Bubeck: Mark, Chicago: Moody, 1975
- † **Overcoming The Adversary**, Bubeck: Mark, Chicago: 1985
- † **The Concise Holman Bible Dictionary**, 1997, 2000
- † **Holman Concise Topical Concordance**, Nashville, Broadman & Holman, 1998
- † **Holman Concise Bible Commentary**, Holman, Broadman & Holman, 1998
- † **Men Mapping Outreach Ministries**, Sterling, KS 2001

† **The Spiritual Man**, Nee: Watchman, New York: Christian Fellowship, 1968

† **Book of Revelation**: Final Frontier, Phinney: Stephen Dr., Exchanging Life, 2007-2013

† **Hebrew Word Pictures**, Seekins: Frank Dr., Phoenix, AZ.: 1998

OTHER TITLES BY STEPHEN PHINNEY:

Book of Prayers: Book, Exchanging Life Publishing

Christian vs. Indwelt Christian: Booklet, Exchanging Life Publishing

Disillusionment of Discipleship: Booklet, IOM America

Doctrinal Check List: Exam, IOM America

Into Thin Air, The Rapture: Booklet, IOM America

Leading Small Groups: Guide Book, IOM America

Living Life Discipleship Manual: Vol. 1 172 pgs, Ministry Tools, Exchanging Life Publishing

Men & Warfare Study Guide: Workbook for Men, Men Mapping Outreach

Sexual Temptations of Man: Workbook for Men, Men Mapping Outreach

Suffering In God's Sovereignty: Booklet, IOM America

The Principled Patriarch: Workbook for Men, IOM America

The Truth About Christmas: Booklet, Exchanging Life Publishing

The Truth Friend: Booklet, IOM America

Dr. Phinney has published over 200 online articles for your review.

Each of these materials can be obtained by logging on to www.iomamerica.org or writing:

IOM America
The Institute of Ministry
P.O. Box 71
Sterling, KS 67579
corporate@iomamerica.org

Printed in Great Britain
by Amazon